OPTICS FOR

THE HUNTER

OPTICS FOR THE HUNTER

John Barsness

Safari Press Inc.
P. O. Box 3095, Long Beach, CA 90803

Barsness, John

Safari Press Inc.

1999, Long Beach, California

ISBN 1-57157-156-6

Library of Congress Catalog Card Number: 98-61446

10 9 8 7 6 5 4 3 2

Readers wishing to receive the Safari Press catalog, featuring many fine books on big-game hunting, wingshooting, and sporting firearms, should write to Safari Press Inc., P.O. Box 3095, Long Beach, CA 90803, USA. Tel: (714) 894-9080 or visit our Web site at: www.safaripress.com.

DEDICATION

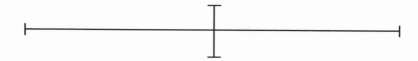

For Bill McRae, who leads the way.

TABLE OF CONTENTS

ACKNOWLEDGMENTS

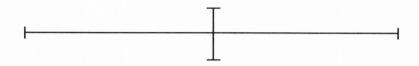

I would like to thank the following folks for their help in offering their knowledge, advice, photographs, products, and sometimes, when we were lucky, good cheer and even campfires:

Larry Weeks of Brownells; Barbara Mellman and Dr. Bill Cross of Bushnell Sports Optics; Pat Beckett of Burris; Terry Moore of Leica; Ray Oeltgen, Gary Williams, Mike Slack, and Forrest Babcock of Leupold; Jim D'Elia of Nikon; Joe Graham, Bob Gerol, Dave Brown and Tony Tekansik of Pentax; Sherry Fears and Allan Jones of Simmons and Weaver; Jim Morey and Rob Fancher of Swarovski; Karen Lutto of Zeiss.

And also: Jay, Bev, Tabitha, and Tiffany Rightnour, for looking through so many binoculars and scopes; Craig Boddington, for getting me into this in the first place; Ludo Wurfbain, for translating the DEVA articles; and Eileen Clarke, for seeming to actually enjoy all those binoculars on the living room windowsill.

INTRODUCTION

HUNTING OPTICS AS A SYSTEM

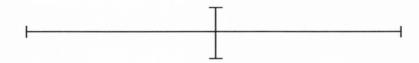

Like many Westerners who like the outdoor life, I've spent some time guiding hunters who come from all over the country to seek the big game of the Rockies and High Plains. This does not, incidentally, make me some sort of expert hunter, because more than half the "guides" out here have been dragged off a barstool, given a bath, and pointed in the right direction on opening morning. But my guiding experiences have shown me how few hunters really understand and know how to use optics.

My first guiding took place during pronghorn season. After we'd fetch our clients from the airport in Billings, the ritual was to let them unpack, then ease their jet-lagged bodies out to the ranch's rifle range, supposedly to make sure their scopes hadn't been torqued in the baggage-toss Olympics.

The real reason was to see if they could actually hit a "prairie goat" at any reasonable range. We had a 15-inch iron gong hung from a wooden frame 250 yards from the benchrest. First, we'd make sure their rifles were sighted-

OPTICS FOR THE HUNTER

in correctly at 100 yards by having them shoot at a paper bull's-eye. Then we'd turn them loose on the gong.

My first two clients weren't untypical. The big guy shot a Browning semiauto in 7mm Remington Magnum, while his small friend had a Sako .243. Both rifles wore first-class glass, the BAR a 3.5–10X Leupold and the Sako a 3–12X Swarovski. I ended up doing the actual sighting-in of the 7mm since the big man evidently couldn't handle the kick of more than two shots in a row. That isn't too unusual either, but after the dust cleared they each hit the gong a time or two. The confidence level was high when we drove out of the ranch yard in the dark the next morning.

By orange light we were up on a hill and looking at 100 square miles of eastern Montana. Soon my 10X Bausch & Lomb binocular found a bunch of antelope over a mile away. "There they are," I said. My clients raised their own binoculars but couldn't even find the herd, much less see the black head of the herd buck. Why? Because both carried identical compact binoculars they'd bought for $39.95 the day before they hit the airport.

I set up the spotting scope and found the herd. My hunters took turns looking and were amazed, since neither had ever looked through a spotting scope before. The buck was good enough, so we went after him. But neither hunter had any idea where the herd was since they'd only seen them through the tiny field of the 30X spotting scope. Before I could guess what he was up to, the larger hunter walked right over the ridge and almost into the herd. They scattered like tan-and-white sparrows.

The rest of the day went downhill. Their tiny, cheap binoculars turned absolutely useless in midday mirage, so they sat around bored while I glassed. Eventually they both got bucks, but I did all the hunting. They left determined to buy better binoculars, and maybe even spotting scopes.

INTRODUCTION

Hunters love to talk calibers, rifles, loads, and even scope sights at length, but we get bored with binoculars. We plot for months and even years over the perfect rifle and scope for every sort of big game from pronghorn to elk to Cape buffalo, and spend thousands of dollars for a rack full of perfect rifles. Then we buy a cheap throwaway binocular at the last moment—if we bother to buy any at all. I still overhear hunters talking about buying a huge variable scope so they "don't have to carry binoculars." I think this tendency is returning with today's craze over supersized scopes for big-game hunting.

It really doesn't matter that you can buy a reasonably portable scope topping out at 12X to 20X and mount it on your .300 magnum. It's still really stupid to use it to look for game. First and foremost, it's dangerous. You should never point a firearm at anything you can't identify beforehand. Say you look through your 4.5–14X variable and find that the movement on the far side of the draw is another hunter—and he's looking right back at you, ticked-off because somebody's pointing a rifle at him. Or maybe your gun goes off while you're looking. Far stranger things happen every day.

Second, it's simply bad hunting. Hunters who use their scopes to "spot" are almost always looking at something they saw with their naked eyes. Nine times out of ten this means the game has seen you first—or surely will when you raise your rifle to look through that scope.

Third, you'll see better through a good 10X binocular than with a 12X or even 15X scope. The reason lies in binocular—which literally means *two-eyed*—vision. A binocular consists of two telescopes side by side, providing a stereoscopic view of the world, giving it depth. The view through a scope is flat and, especially at the higher magnifications of today's big variables, dimmer than through a good binocular.

3

(Binocular, by the way, is the correct term. I know we're used to saying "a pair of binoculars," but the *bi* in binocular already means a pair of something. Saying you're looking through a pair of *binoculars* is like saying you're riding a pair of bicycles. I point this out not to sound snooty but because I don't want you to think I'm weird when I use the term binocular throughout this book. I am no weirder than the average writer, which may not be saying much, but I'll probably screw up somewhere in here and say binoculars when I mean binocular anyway, so don't hold it against me. With persistence you'll get used to reading binocular even if you never say it.)

Over the years I also found that most hunting writers, like most hunters, don't know much about optics either. I read a whole bunch of articles on the topic, but they all seemed remarkably the same. Most talked about the various sorts of aberrations present in optical systems. Talking about barrel or pincushion aberrations, or achromatic versus apochromatic lenses, may provide the illusion that the author understands the technical side of optics, but it never did me a bit of good when picking out scopes or binoculars. (Right there I am talking about more than one binocular, so adding an *s* is correct.)

So I started learning about optics myself, first through my friend Bill McRae, who was the first hunting writer ever to really delve into optics, and to whom this book is dedicated. Then I lucked into a job at *Petersen's Hunting* magazine. Its then-editor, Craig Boddington, had decided to start an optics column and offered it to Bill McRae. He was too busy and suggested me. I wrote Craig a list of what I'd write about in the first year's columns and got the job. That went on for six years, during which I learned a great deal about optics through many friends in the hunting optics industry, and by talking to hundreds of people who use optics professionally—from gunsmiths to Alaskan guides to professional hunters in Africa. The list is too long to give thanks to everyone, but I would like to thank Craig Boddington for the opportunity to learn on the job.

During the period I was working for *Petersen's Hunting*, I found that very few hunters regard hunting optics as a system. Instead they like to think only about their riflescope, and maybe secondarily about binoculars or (very rarely) a spotting scope.

A scope sight is designed for aiming. Binoculars are for looking. The function of an optical system is to find and shoot game, and this is most efficiently done by using your binocular for finding and your scope for aiming. I'd much rather hunt the world over with one rifle equipped with a 4X scope and a really good 8X or 10X binocular than with half a dozen rifles chambered for everything from the .25-06 Remington to the .458 Winchester and no binocular at all.

I can back up that statement with an example from what TV personalities might call real life. In my years as a big-game hunter and writer, I've experimented with a wide variety of rifles and scopes. I've killed big game on three continents, using rifles chambered for several dozen calibers ranging from the .220 Swift to the .375 Holland & Holland Magnum. The scopes ranged from fixed 2.5X models to variables topping out at 10X, and the size of the game ranged from 40-pound javelina to 1,400-pound moose.

While I was fiddling around, my wife hunted with a couple of .270s—first a Browning A-Bolt and then an Ultra Light Arms Model 24. She started with a 4X Bushnell but today uses a 2–7X Bausch & Lomb, though why I don't know since she almost never turns it off 4X. Her game has included a number of pronghorns, including one buck taken with a heart shot at 450 yards, several good mule and white-tailed deer, elk, and moose. The moose was her tenth, one-shot kill in a row.

Admittedly, she did this all in Montana, and not across the world. I will not claim that a .270 with a 4X scope is all you need for every big-game animal in North America, but I will note that when Eileen got that A-Bolt she also received a 7X35 Nikon binocular. Later she graduated to a couple of Zeisses, an 8X compact for steep country and an 8X56 Night Owl for more level ground. Rather than charging across the countryside, she prefers to move slowly or sit still in prime game country and patiently look through those glasses. Then she places one sure shot at unalarmed game. Most of the men I've guided could learn a lot from that. Soon she will go to Africa, seeking big game ranging from warthog and impala to wildebeest and zebra. She will take her .270 and her little Zeiss binocular, and I am willing to bet serious money that she will return with everything she sets out to find.

What all this boils down to is priorities. Because of what I do for a living, I have far more rifles and optics than I really need, but most of us must limit what we spend on hunting gear. If I was starting all over with a budget of $1,000, I'd buy a used bolt-action rifle in some all-round caliber such as .30-06 for $300, a really good riflescope of 4X or maybe 3–9X for $200, a decent full-size Porro-prism binocular of 7X or 8X for $250, and a decent variable-power spotting scope, also for around $250.

Those optics prices are realistic in 1998 if you shop around a little, especially by mail-order catalog. In this book I'll tell you how to decide, all by yourself, just what scopes and binoculars are "decent" optically—and why sheer optical quality is not the only measure of a hunter's optics. You will not read anything about pincushion distortion, though you *will* read about some other kinds of optical failings that are much more common and, more importantly, actually relevant to hunting optics.

One last note: I feel almost naked out in the woods without a binocular, even when I'm not hunting. There's so much more to see out there when you carry some glass eyes. Carrying a binocular into the mountain or plains— or even every time you get in the pickup for a drive—helps you to see the natural world more clearly, to find those distant particles of movement that turn into deer at the edge of the cottonwoods or an eagle swooping over a rabbit. Through binoculars we can eavesdrop on the wild and, so, become more a part of what we hunt. Of course, we'll see other things too—a blue jay chasing a red squirrel, a flock of mallards falling like leaves into a prairie pothole, perhaps even a wolverine digging on a distant talus slope— and they will all bring us knowledge and pleasure. Those, too, are valuable things.

Most of all, learning to use optics will make us better and safer hunters, and that is the intention of this book—an aid to help the hunters of the world.

PART ONE

TELESCOPIC SIGHTS

BRIGHT
SCOPES

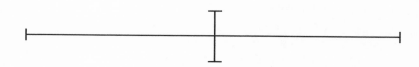

It's difficult for today's hunter to imagine the contro-
versies that once swirled around scope sights. Many British
sportsmen considered the early scopes unsporting because
they felt scopes provided the hunter with an unfair advantage over the game. In America, hunters thought them
delicate and unreliable contraptions. Most pre-World War
II literature on hunting rifles suggested that scopes be
backed up by good iron sights in case the scope cracked,
fogged, or started pointing toward the magnetic north rather
than the deer at hand.

Today's hunters never consider such issues. We know
that scopes are safer than iron sights, allowing us to see
whether our intended target is indeed a deer or some wit-
less human wearing a brown jacket. And we've decided
that scopes are actually more ethical, allowing us to aim
more precisely, which helps us take game cleanly and hu-
manely. Our scopes are so reliable that we consider hunting
rifles incomplete without one. In fact, we even use scopes

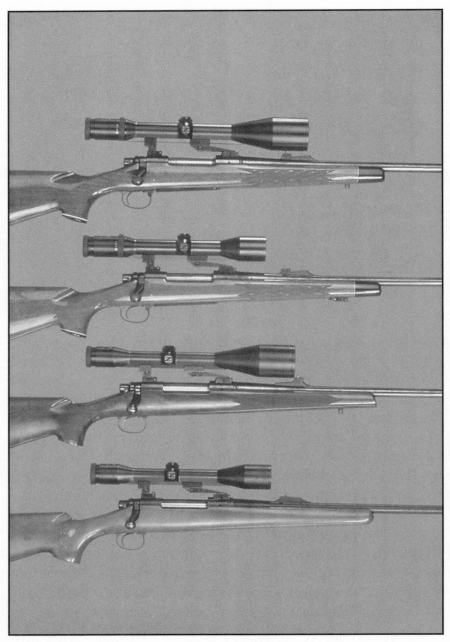

Many European scopes, like these Zeiss models, feature large objective lenses because Europeans often hunt at night.

during "primitive" hunting seasons on our stainless-steel, synthetic-stocked muzzleloaders.

Despite their common use, there's still some confusion about what makes a good hunting scope. Optical brightness has become the big selling point. Some hunters call this clarity (as in, "Gosh, this is a clear scope"), while optical technicians talk about high light transmission. I'll use the term brightness because the world looks brighter through a good scope, elevating our spirits through high contrast and true color, especially in dim light.

But why is brightness seen as the only criterion, especially in North America, where every state and Canadian province outlaws night hunting for big game? To fulfill their purpose of aiming, scopes must also be fogproof, tough enough to take hard recoil, and remain far enough from our face during recoil that a .338 Winchester Magnum doesn't drive the rear lens into our supraorbital ridge. A good hard whack in the eyebrow not only hurts like hell but bleeds like roadkill. Neither promotes accurate shooting.

Some scopes of outstanding optical brightness won't stand up to the repeated recoil of a .220 Swift, will fog at the merest whisper of Alaska, or will perform a crude frontal lobotomy when mounted on any rifle that kicks harder than a light .270. In the best of all possible worlds, this would not be so, but there it is. We'll look at all the other desirable qualities of hunting scopes in due time, but for the moment we'll scrutinize brightness—partly because that's what you'll notice first about any good quality optic and partly because the whole discussion will help when we talk about binoculars and spotting scopes.

After all, the optical qualities of a scope sit there right in front of our eyes every time we pick up a rifle. We can peer through the scope and instantly see brightness, even when it's not easy to see (and sometimes impossible to evaluate) anything else. Nobody ever picks up a rifle, looks through the scope, and says, "Boy, what great eye relief!" Instead they aim the rifle at a window, and if the optics are halfway decent, they exclaim, "What a bright scope!"

Here's a secret: Just about any scope looks really good at high noon on a sunny day. Look out a picture window with the cheapest Korean-made $29.95 special sold in bubble-pack down at Wal-Mart and then a $1,000 Zeiss, and you won't see much difference. But try placing them side by side when the sun sinks behind the nearest ridge. With the Zeiss you'll be able to peer into the dark draws and see deer; with the "affordable" glass you'll see dark draws. That difference will grow as the last legal minutes of shooting light slide away.

An often overlooked factor affects the brightness of even the best scopes. About ten years ago I hunted white-tailed deer on White Oak Plantation in southern Alabama. The routine at White Oak, and most other southern hunting lodges, is to sit in stands morning and evening, maybe rattling or grunting a little to attract a deer.

Like whitetails anywhere, most White Oak bucks are shot in early morning or late evening, so a bright scope is a practical hunting tool. One day after lunch we sat around on the porch looking at each other's scopes. My .270 wore a 3–9X Bausch & Lomb Balvar; the other rifles wore a wide variety of scopes, ranging from high-priced Leupolds and Burrises to really affordable Simmonses and Tascos. All were judged adequate, except by one big fellow from Louisiana.

This guy had a .300 Weatherby Magnum wearing a 3–12X Swarovski with a 30mm tube. "Humph," he said after looking at the others. "Now, *this* is a bright scope." He handed me the rifle, and I turned it toward the field behind the lodge, looking into the shadows of the oak timber two hundred yards away. The view didn't look very bright;

in fact, it appeared pretty dim. I took the rifle off my shoulder and looked at the scope's rear lens, which was coated with a thin layer of dust. Turning the rifle around, I looked at the front lens. More particles of Mississippi Delta mud. "Sure is bright," I said, handing it back. He nodded, nose angled upward.

Rule Number One of bright scopes is: Clean them often. The finest optics don't work any better than the worst when dusty or rain-spotted.

Two factors commonly thought to affect scope brightness are 30mm tubes and big objective lenses. In reality, magnification and lens quality have more effect, but

The most abundant and probably the most nocturnal big-game animal in North America is the white-tailed deer. Bright optics can make a real difference when hunting whitetails.

since so many shooters get duped into buying big scopes, thinking they'll be able to spot black bears in Carlsbad Cavern, let's look at the other factors first.

A few years ago some advertising guys got together and decided that since those pricey, super-bright European scopes mostly use 30mm tubes and big objective lenses, then the big tubes and objective lenses must be what make things bright. Some compared 56mm objectives and 30mm tubes to water funnels. Just as a big funnel allows more water flow, they figured, a big scope allows more light to strike your eye.

They were about half right. There's a big flaw in this analogy. Light passing through any telescope isn't funneled down by the scope tube but by the lenses. You can observe this fact by holding a scope at arm's length and noting the small circle of light in the center of the ocular lens. This circle, as you may know, is called the *exit pupil*, the source of the image we see when we lean forward and aim our rifle. The exit pupil's size—especially its diameter—is critical to a scope's brightness.

The reason lies in our own eyes. The pupils of our eyes expand in dim light and contract in bright light, controlling the amount of light that strikes the rods and cones at the rear of our eyeballs. These rods and cones send an image to our brain, which is the reason we can see.

In very dim light, the pupils of a young adult's eyes will open to 7mm, or close to it. In using optics, this means two things: First, for a scope to provide all the brightness possible, its exit pupil should approach 7mm. Secondly, an exit pupil bigger than 7mm is "wasted." Say you're using a funnel to fill a bottle. If you pour water faster than the funnel can handle, the funnel fills up and water slops over the edges, never making it into the bottle. The same thing happens with excess light from an oversize exit pupil—it slops over the sides of your pupil and never makes it inside your eye.

The diameter of a scope's exit pupil depends on three factors: One is the magnification of the scope since more magnification means a smaller exit pupil. Everything else being equal, an 8X scope will have an exit pupil half the diameter of a 4X scope's. Second is the diameter of the objective lens. This lens "scoops" light into the scope. A 40mm objective lens on a 4X scope results in an exit pupil twice the diameter of the same scope with a 20mm lens. Third is the interior of the scope itself. If the inside of the scope

Ray Allen took this nice whitetail with the aid of a big Swarovski scope, a perfect glass for low-light stand hunting.

The brightest scope for the dollar is a fixed 6X, like the 6X36 M8 Leupold on this custom Mauser in .257 Roberts. Even variable scopes are typically brightest when set at 6X or slightly more, but since fixed-power scopes have fewer lenses, they're slightly brighter than variables.

restricts the light passing through the lenses, then the exit pupil shrinks.

A scope's exit pupil diameter can be found in two ways. Normally, the easiest way is to divide the diameter of the objective lens by the magnification of the scope. A 6X scope with a 42mm objective has a 7mm exit pupil (42÷6=7). Consequently, the size of a variable scope's exit pupil will change as we turn the magnification ring up or down. A 3–10X variable with the same 42mm objective lens will have a 14mm exit pupil at 3X (42÷3=14) and a 4.2mm exit pupil at 10X (42÷10= 4.2).

The second way is to measure the exit pupil with a small ruler or caliper. This isn't as easy as it sounds, because you must point the scope toward a light source, then hold it still while measuring that little dot of light. Although difficult to do, this is indeed the way to test whether a 30mm tube actually transmits more light than a 1-inch tube. If the exit pupil is smaller than predicted by the objective lens/magnification formula, then obviously something inside the scope is restricting the flow of light. I tried this myself one afternoon by sitting on my living room couch with several variable scopes.

First, I compared a Zeiss 2.5–10X with a 48mm objective lens and a 30mm tube with a Leupold 3.5–10X with a 50mm objective and 1-inch tube. The objective sizes were matched closely enough to ignore, so if I found any significant difference in exit pupil sizes, it had to be due to the 30mm tube.

Both scopes had the same size exit pupil at any magnification above 5X. Below 5X, the Zeiss did have a slightly larger exit pupil. But at 5X the exit pupil of a scope with a 48mm objective is almost 10mm, far larger than needed to transmit all the light our eyes can use anyway.

What this means is that by the time any variable scope is cranked up to 5X or 6X, tube diameter (and interior lens size) doesn't affect the size of the exit pupil. The reason so many 30mm European scopes have a reputation for brightness is not their 30mm tube but their excellent multi-coated glass. If you compare a low-priced 1-inch-tubed Pacific Rim scope with a 30mm Zeiss or Swarovski, the cheap scope places a very distant second. But if you compare a 1-inch Zeiss or Swarovski (or a 1-inch Leupold Vari-X III or Pentax Lightseeker) with a 30mm Zeiss or Swarovski, you won't be able to tell any difference—unless the objective lenses are different sizes, which creates larger exit pupils.

The real reason Europeans make 30mm tubes has nothing to do with optical brightness. Europe uses the metric system, and that's the tube size they standardized years ago. Just as we chose 1-inch after experimenting with $3/4$-inch, $7/8$-inch, and even 26mm and 26.5mm tubes.

A bigger objective lens does make a scope brighter—but only at magnifications above 6X to 7X. And not by all that much. At the highest magnification of most hunting variables—say, 10X—a 50mm objective gives us a 5mm exit pupil, while a 42mm objective provides a 4.2mm pupil—not much difference.

As we get older, a larger exit pupil makes less difference in a scope's apparent brightness. As noted earlier, 7mm is the maximum young eyes attain in extremely dim light. By the time our beltline expands and our ear hair starts growing out of control (sometime in our 40s), our pupils can reach a maximum of only about 6mm. The maximum shrinks about a millimeter each decade after that—the reason your grandfather didn't like to drive at night. His pupils didn't open up to more than 4mm, and he simply couldn't see as well as he used to.

As we grow older, good glass and multi-coated lenses make much more difference in scope brightness than a large objective lens, and they even make a significant difference when we're younger. When I test optics for brightness, I do not rely only on my 45-year-old and possibly prejudiced eyes, but often have friends stand beside me to make the same tests. These range from teenagers to Social Security retirees.

I make these tests at dusk, often looking at actual deer—an illuminating experience (pun definitely intended). Over the years I've compared many scopes, and in the past couple of years I have made a conscious effort to compare variable hunting scopes topping out around 10X, since these are the biggest sellers. Here's a sampling of 1-inch-tubed scopes that have passed through the house recently, from dimmest to brightest:

- Tasco Bighorn 2.5–10X50
- Weaver V10 2–10X38
- Kahles 2.2–9X42
- Leupold Vari-X II 3–9X40
- Simmons 2.8–10X44
- Nikon Monarch UCC 3–9X40
- Bausch & Lomb 2.5–10X40
- Pentax Lightseeker 3–11X43

—and the last three, in a tie:

- Swarovski 3–10X42 A
- Leupold 3.5–10X40 Vari-X III
- Zeiss 3–9X36 MC

The first two numbers are the magnification range of each scope, the last number (after the X) the diameter of the objective lens. Please remember that these findings represent an average of subjective observations by several observers. We looked through all the scopes both at maximum magnification and at 6X, and sometimes one scope would do better at 6X than at the maximum. Sometimes there was disagreement among the observers, especially in the middle of the pack. The three brightest scopes all ended up in a virtual dead heat.

Also, manufacturers are constantly fiddling with their product, and many scope makers don't produce their own lenses. Instead they order them from a subcontractor or, sometimes, several subcontractors. A scope made in 1996 may be slightly brighter or dimmer than one made in 1997, and a scope made in 1987 or 1977 will probably not be as bright as one made today, even if the model and overall mechanics remain the same.

Some notes on the scopes themselves:

The Tasco Bighorn is one of the company's highest-priced scopes. I included it mostly to show that a 50mm objective is not all there is to brightness, as many folks believe. This scope was noticeably dimmer than the Weaver to all observers, despite the huge objective. I will discuss exactly why at length later on.

The Weaver is by far the trimmest and lightest (11½ ounces) of all the scopes, and pretty darn bright for having the smallest objective.

The Kahles just goes to show that all European scopes are not created equal. It is noticeably brighter than the first two scopes, but noticeably dimmer than any top-line Japanese scope. I have tested more than one Kahles, and this one did not surprise.

The Leupold Vari-X IIs are Leupold's less expensive variables. The primary difference lies in optics, not scope construction.

The Simmons Aetec line is one of the brightest for the buck in the business. At 15½ ounces, it's also the heaviest scope listed. All observers rated it noticeably brighter than the Kahles, and a touch above the Leupold.

The next three were very close together; in fact, some observers would have reversed the order for two or more of the scopes:

The Nikon is from the new Monarch line made in Thailand. There was some concern among Nikon fans about this shift in venues, but this test scope seems as bright as the Japanese-made models.

The Bausch & Lomb is from the firm's top-of-the-line 4000 series; the lower-priced 3000s are not quite as bright.

I frankly expected the Pentax to rank with the next group, because I've tested its Lightseeker series before and they usually match up very well. But this particular scope was definitely just a notch below the very brightest, perhaps because it was the only scope tested with an adjustable objective. More on that later, as well.

As noted, the Swarovski, Leupold, and Zeiss scopes all ended up in a virtual dead heat. To get this kind of brightness you simply must pay for it. In a 1997 Redhead catalog (the hunting division of Bass Pro Shops), I

The author tested a number of scopes, using other people to help sort the dim from the bright.

The size of the objective lens, along with quality of glass and coatings, determines brightness of a given scope.

found the Leupold for $415, the Zeiss for $500, and the Swarovski for $530.

What this particular test indicated is that lens quality, not huge objectives, is the primary factor in scope brightness. The scopes at the top of the heap all use fully multi-coated optics.

A more scientific test was done by DEVA, which is an acronym for a quasi-governmental German organization that tests firearms, ammo, and shooting-related products. In 1993 it ran a number of tests on various European, American, and Pacific Rim scopes, some of the tests involving light transmission. One comparative test involved small variables (*Druckjagdglaser fur den flinken Schuss*, which according to my translator and publisher, Ludo Wurfbain, means "scopes for driven game hunts on rifles of hefty caliber.") Here's how some scopes familiar (at least in name) and available to North American hunters ranked in light transmitted, again from dimmest to brightest:

Table 1.1

SCOPE	DAYLIGHT	TWILIGHT
Tasco 1–3.5X20	78.8%	75.1%
Docter 1–4X24	82.8%	77.1%
Bushnell 1.5–4.5X21	84.8%	80.4%
Kahles 1.1–4.5X20	88.9%	83.3%
Schmidt & Bender 1.25–4X20	88.9%	85.9%
Swarovski 1.5–4.5X20	91.0%	87.7%
Leupold 1.5–5X20 Vari-X III	91.6%	91.1%
Zeiss 1.25–4X24	94.5%	92.9%

Again, these were scientific tests using fine instruments, some loaned by Schmidt & Bender and Zeiss, including a *spektral photo meter*. For all of that, they don't seem to differ much from my tests, made through the eyes of various humans, given that not all the same scopes were involved.

Another test involved larger variables topping out at 10X to 12X. Once more the rankings are from dimmest to brightest, though here the DEVA folks rounded off the percentage of transmitted light:

Table 1.2

SCOPE	DAYLIGHT	TWILIGHT
Tasco 3-12X52	81%	78%
Docter 2.5–10X48	84%	80%
Schmidt & Bender 3–12X	89%	87%
Swarovski 3–12X56	91%	87%
Redfield 4–12X	92%	91%
Leupold 3.5–10X50	94%	92%
Zeiss 2.5–10X48	94%	92%

Apparently, there is not as much magic in European lenses as many of us would like to believe.

Interestingly, the small-variable DEVA tests also included a "quality of picture" ranking, which was subjective in that several individuals looked through all the scopes and

Despite much advertising hype, 30mm tubes don't allow more light to pass through the scope. If they did, the exit pupil would be larger. This photo was taken looking through the exit pupils of a 1-inch-tubed Swarovski variable (left) and a 30mm-tubed Zeiss variable (right). Both are set at 6X, and there's no discernible difference in the size of the exit pupil. Only at the very lowest magnifications (under 4X) will a 30mm tube have a bigger exit pupil—but at those magnifications the exit pupil is far larger than the eye can use anyway.

rated the view in terms of contrast and brilliance. Here the Leupold 1.5–5X, which finished a very narrow second to the Zeiss on the spektral photo meter, was somehow rated "mediocre." Something tells me a little German prejudice was at work here, though when the bigger variables were tested the Leupold 3.5–10X was given very high rankings in the subjective test. (I will also cite other results from the DEVA tests in later chapters.)

My own experience indicates that although color rendition may not be quite so accurate in one bright scope as in another, when you get a lot of light coming through the scope the image always has good contrast. Also, though not noted by DEVA, many of the European scopes featured 30mm tubes. There was no brightness advantage evident for 30mm tubes in either test.

Coated lenses were developed by Zeiss back in the late 1930s, when one of its optical engineers noticed that some older binoculars and scopes seemed brighter than the newer ones. He then noticed that the old scopes had a blue-green tint on their lenses. Chemical analysis proved this to be magnesium fluoride, one of the ingredients of the company's optical glass. Further analysis suggested that the compound was leaching out of the glass over time. But why did it make the lenses brighter?

When light strikes uncoated glass, only about half the rays pass through. The rest are reflected back into the atmosphere. Eventually it was found that the extremely thin coating of magnesium fluoride on the old lenses was about half the length of an average wave of light. When stray light bounces off the glass underneath a coating, most is reflected back through the lens by the surface of the coating—and hence toward our eye.

The fact that the coating is about half a wavelength thick is important. If the coating were a whole wavelength in depth, the light waves would still tend to reflect off the lens. Half-wave coatings, however, "catch" more light than they allow to escape. Light transmission through single-coated lenses is usually around 85 to 90 percent, rather than the 50 to 60 percent of uncoated glass.

Soon the Zeiss folks figured out how to deliberately apply a coating of magnesium fluoride. (If you really want to know, it's through molecular bombardment in a vacuum. This makes about as much difference to me as the fact that computers have chips. If you can't eat the chips, or get bombarded by your scope, who cares?) These first lenses were single-coated, with only one layer of coating.

But light, as a few of you are already protesting, is not made of just one wavelength—the reason we see different colors. Each color has its own frequency, just as high and low sounds have different frequencies. Soon it was found that extra layers of other compounds could catch light waves that single-coated lenses allowed to escape. Lenses with more than one coating are called, naturally, multi-coated. Today's best multi-coated lenses transmit about 99 percent of available light.

One catch, of course, is that there's multi-coating and then there's multi-coating. Technically, two layers qualify. The top optics manufacturers use three or four coatings, and Pentax uses seven, a system adapted from the windows in the space shuttle.

Also, the top makers multi-coat all lens surfaces, while often on cheaper scopes only one or two surfaces are multi-coated. The Tasco Bighorn listed in my tests, for instance, has only the objective lens multi-coated, while all the other lenses are single-coated.

Some scopes are fully single-coated throughout, which means single coating on all lens surfaces. That's the big difference between the Leupold Vari-X II and III lines; the IIs are single-coated while the IIIs feature a very good multi-coating. The difference in brightness is significant. Perhaps more important is what happens when a single-coated scope is aimed toward the sun—as often happens at sunrise or sunset. At those times, the flare of light off the lenses can wash out the image. But with good multi-coating, flare is almost entirely eliminated, and you are able to see and aim.

The more lenses you have in a scope, the less light gets through. If each multi-coated lens in a scope transmits 99 percent of available light, a 6-lens scope will transmit 94 percent of available light, while a 10-lens scope will transmit only 90 percent. Variables and adjustable-objective scopes have more lenses, which is why the 3–11X Pentax Lightseeker isn't as bright as some other Pentaxs or the top three scopes in our test. This is also why some variable scopes from the same manufacturer are brighter than others, and why fixed-power scopes (which use fewer lenses) can be brighter than variables.

The inside of a good scope must also be painted or baffled with some sort of antireflection system. It doesn't do any good to let all that light through good glass only to have it bounce around inside the scope and not reach your eye. Like good glass and precise multi-coating, this costs money. I suspect it's the reason the single-coated Leupold Vari-X II line is brighter than some multi-coated scopes.

Also, a few scopes feature a field stop, an interior blocking of the light that actually shrinks the exit pupil. Why in the hell would they do that, you ask? Well, a field stop works like the aperture in a camera lens, which sharpens the image by cutting down on diffraction.

Diffraction is light that doesn't end up in the middle of the image. Diffracted light fuzzes the image and is mostly caused by light coming in around the edges of the lens. A field stop resembles a large washer inside the scope tube. It blocks the light around the edges of the image, improving sharpness.

A field stop also reduces exit pupil size considerably. So you have a trade-off in which you get a sharper but dimmer image. It's an inexpensive way of increasing image sharpness in cheap scopes; I don't know of any good scopes that use field stops.

You can tell if a scope features a field stop by measuring the exit pupil. Curious about why that Tasco Bighorn was so dim in spite of its 50mm objective, I placed a metric ruler across the exit pupil. Sure enough, at 6X the diameter was about 6mm, instead of measuring over 8mm ($50 \div 6 = 8.3$).

By reversing our equation, we can figure out that a 6mm exit pupil at 6X magnification requires a 36mm objective. Due to the field stop, the Bighorn's objective lens is effectively reduced to 36mm. No wonder the scope is so dim, despite its huge objective lens.

After all these tests were done, I threw a few other scopes into the equation, from fixed 6Xs to 30mm versions of the Swarovski and Zeiss. The fixed 6Xs from Weaver, Leupold, Swarovski, and Zeiss were slightly but noticeably brighter than the variables from the same manufacturer set at 6X. I tested two Leupold 6Xs, their single-coated 6X36 and their fully multi-coated 6X42. The 6X42 is of course brighter, due to both the bigger objective and the multi-coating, but the 6X36 is also very bright, almost as bright as the 6X32 Zeiss. The 6X38 K6 Weaver is also quite bright and, like the Simmons Aetec, one of the better brightness bargains in the business. If you need a bright scope and also want it to be light and affordable, a fixed 6X fills the bill.

Swarovski makes a 2.5–10X42 in 30mm, and if there is any difference in brightness between it and the company's 1-inch "American-style" 3–10X42, none of us could see it. It's just bigger, heavier, and costs twice as much.

If you feel you need extra brightness, go to a bigger front lens. For about $100 more, Swarovski makes the same 30mm scope with a 56mm objective, which is brighter. The Zeiss 2.5–10X48 was also slightly brighter than the 3–9X36, but again, it costs more than twice as much. I also tested a 3.5–10X50 Steiner Hunting Z, and it ranked about with the Leupold Vari-X II and Simmons Aetec. As with the Kahles, this did not surprise. Steiner has a few decent if not great binoculars in its line, but overall its optical quality does not match up well with the other well-known German brands such as Leica and Zeiss.

Obviously, the secret to buying bright scopes lies partly in spending money—but just because some European scopes run twice the price of top-of-the-line American and Japanese scopes doesn't mean they're twice as bright. European scopes are often inflated by the high wages demanded by strong trade unions as well as the U.S. import duties applied to all optics. For these reasons, Leica, Steiner, Swarovski, and Zeiss are now making scopes over here.

(As I'm writing this, Swarovski and Zeiss are assembling only one model scope in American subsidiary plants, while Steiner's Hunting Z and Leica's whole line are manufactured by Leupold, with only the lenses coming from Germany. If more Americans buy these less-expensive scopes, I'm sure we'll see more models appear.)

Within limits, a high price tag is an indicator of the optical quality inside a scope. For my own use, I have never found a scope costing more than around $500 to be worth the extra money.

Note that I haven't yet mentioned the concepts of relative brightness or twilight factor in this treatise. Relative brightness is a term you may see in some older catalogs and articles about optics. Though still occasionally mentioned by hunting writers who don't know any better, it's been mostly dropped because it had nothing to do with reality, so I won't bore you with its equation. It indicated that low-powered scopes were brighter than higher-magnification models. Anybody who looks through a 2.5X scope and a 6X scope at dusk can see this isn't true.

Twilight factor, however, does bear some relationship to reality, mostly by acknowledging the role magnification plays in scope brightness. The closer we get to anything in dim light—a signpost, deer, or saloon—the better we can see it. This is true whether we walk closer, drive a Lexus closer, or use magnifying optics.

The equation for twilight factor accounts for both magnification and exit pupil diameter. To find a scope's twilight factor, multiply its magnification by objective lens diameter, then find the square root of that number. For example, a standard 4X scope with a 28mm objective has a twilight factor of 10.6 (the square root of 4X28), while a 6X42 has a twilight factor of 15.9 (the square root of 6X42).

Within the limits of most hunting scopes up to about 8X and given equal glass and coatings, this tends to work out pretty well. I just tested a 10-year-old Bausch & Lomb Balfor, one of the brightest 4X scopes I've ever seen, against a Leupold 2–7X Vari-X II Compact. The 4X has a 32mm objective and multi-coated lenses, the 2–7X a 28mm objective and single coating. Most optical advantages should lie with the 4X scope—multi-coating, larger exit pupil, the fewer lenses of a fixed-power scope. Even so, the Leupold set at 7X was just slightly brighter. This is entirely due to magnification, the really important part of twilight factor.

Moving closer helps you see better only with a 5mm to 7mm exit pupil. With a 50mm objective, 8X is about all the magnification that helps, depending on your age. At that power, the small field of view becomes a problem, and the scopes need to be mounted very high. For big-game hunting, most of us (especially when over 40) are better off with objective lenses of around 40mm. These allow all the light we really need for shooting American-style, even in tall timber at the last moment of legal light on a cloudy day. I know, because that's when I shot my last bull elk—with the help of a Bausch & Lomb 1.5–6X set on 6X. This is contrary to the old idea that timber scopes should be low-powered, since it's actually higher magnification that helps you see better in dim light. The only disadvantage is a smaller field of view, but an average 6X provides a field of four feet at twenty-five yards. If you can't find a deer or elk in that, you're simply not very good at pointing your rifle.

By the way, I carefully cleaned the lenses of all those scopes before we looked through them. That's perhaps the biggest trick involved. Remember it, and you'll see a long way into the shadows.

RELIABLE
SCOPES

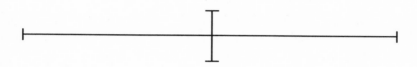

The world's greatest lenses can help us see across high plains canyons or into shadowed timber. But those fine optics can't help if the scope fogs, the reticle breaks, or the dang thing won't remain sighted-in for more than a few shots.

Recoil causes most scope breakdowns, and its effects are cumulative. Enough shots from any center-fire rifle, handgun, or shotgun will take apart any scope. A sturdy scope on a .22 rimfire may last for 100,000 shots, while lesser scopes may go to pieces after ten rounds from a .300 Weatherby, a 12-gauge slug gun, or a .44 Magnum pistol (which despite what Dirty Harry says is a long way from the "world's most powerful handgun"). But no scope can withstand the forces of recoil forever and ever.

Oddly enough, most scopes can't even survive life on "BB guns." I put that common term in quotes because many of today's airguns, especially target arms, are masterpieces of the gunmaker's craft, as precise as any powder-burning rifle. To an adult human, they seem to have no recoil, but the springs and pistons that make airguns shoot create all sorts of weird vibrations—and not the kind you feel at night in some strange city. Those vibrations can shake apart an ordinary scope within one-hundred shots.

The reason? Most scopes are designed to withstand the backward thrust of center-fire recoil, but an air gun vibrates in every direction. Special scopes, therefore, must be designed and built for airguns.

Even some modern center-fire rifles can cause problems with standard scopes. My friend Melvin Forbes builds hunting rifles at his Ultra Light Arms factory in Granville, West Virginia. Many Ultra Lights weigh less than 6 pounds with scope. Light weight increases recoil, but that alone doesn't kill scopes. Muzzle brakes do the job.

Muzzle brakes take the gas that leaves the muzzle and deflect it to the side and, often, slightly to the rear. This keeps our shoulder intact, but on a 5-pound rifle the gases can actually jerk a rifle forward slightly at the end of the recoil cycle.

The best modern scopes have one-piece tubes made out of aircraft-grade aluminum. These have a slight advantage over scopes with objective and eyepiece bells threaded on separately. They are also lighter and less likely to damage interior parts than steel tubes.

Like the strange vibrations of an air gun, this opposite jerk can take scopes apart in a hurry. Every year Melvin gets calls complaining about the lousy groups from somebody's brand-new Ultra Light 7mm Magnum. Melvin usually asks what kind of scope he's using. The customer answers huffily that he's using a such-and-such, usually a pretty good scope. (People who buy $2,500 rifles can afford good scopes.) Melvin calmly suggests that the customer try a new scope, or a brand he knows can stand the shock, such as Leupold. Just about every time, a new scope fixes the problem.

It's sad to say this, but it seems to me there were fewer problems with scopes twenty-odd years ago. I was in my mid-twenties then and, like most twenty-somethings, didn't have a lot of money, so I bought inexpensive scopes. They seemed to hold up very well, while many of today's less expensive scopes—and even some fairly expensive models—simply don't.

Part of the reason is that today's hunters are using lightweight rifles chambered for more powerful cartridges. Thirty years ago the .30-06 was considered a big rifle, and the average Winchester or Remington so chambered weighed close to ten pounds with scope. Today many hunters are carrying .300 magnums weighing under eight pounds scoped.

Over the same period, scopes grew. Many hip, modern hunters seem to feel that anything less than a 4–12X isn't big enough for deer. Combine lighter, harder-kicking rifles with heavier scopes, and the more the scope will tend to stay put while the rifle backs up. This pounding causes more breakdowns, so more shooters send scopes back for repair. We find then more manufacturers beef up their scopes, often using heavier materials. In the long run I'm not really sure this helps. Leupold, the brand with perhaps the best reputation for being recoil-proof, builds scopes as light as anybody's. I suspect this lightness is one of the reasons for the reputation.

But I also suspect the big reason scopes held up better thirty years ago is that most manufacturers were still fighting the "scopes are delicate" reputation passed down from prewar hunters. So even low-priced scopes were built tough—and you could buy a lot more Japanese scope for a few dollars in 1960 than you can today.

As example is the 2.5X Bushnell scope on John Van Der Meulen's .458 Winchester. These days John is a South African game rancher, but prior to that he was a professional control shooter for many years in Rhodesia (now Zimbabwe). In that job he killed thousands of Cape buffalo and elephant with various big rifles, but mostly he used the .458 that he still owns. It still wears that 2.5X Bushnell it wore in Rhodesia, and the scope still works fine.

I don't think you could get more than fifty or one hundred shots out of most of today's less-expensive scopes on a rifle suitable for elephant control. I say this because I've tried many of them on rifles chambered for magnums from .300 to .416. But there is still no hard-and-fast rule about price versus strength. My wife has a Bushnell 4X scope mounted on the rifled-barrel Mossberg 12-gauge pump gun she bought for hunting whitetails in a nearby shotgun-only area. Before that she had it on a smooth-tubed Remington 870 used for the same purpose. To me, a light 12-gauge shooting 3-inch slug loads kicks worse than any .375 H&H Magnum I've ever fired, but this sub-$100 scope has never flinched.

That particular Bushnell is from the company's discontinued Scopechief line. Today there are three or four grades of Bushnell scopes, but the company's very best scopes carry the Bausch & Lomb name—an old American company that bought out Bushnell awhile back. The old Bushnell Scopechief line evolved into the B&L Scopechief, then finally the B&L Elite 3000.

Could any of the new Bushnells make it on a .458? Maybe, since the firm sells some models designed for slug use. But I'd also guess the Bushnells sold in blister packs at K-Mart

When hunting Alaskan brown bear, your scope had better be completely waterproof. Many costly European scopes aren't since their adjustment turrets aren't sealed.

won't be as tough. Most other makers of "affordable" scopes have similar lines ranging from very cheap to middle-range.

In 1960 hunters were just beginning to accept scopes, so any scope might be mounted on a .243 to a .458. Today everybody uses scopes, and the less expensive brands simply don't need to be as tough since most folks aren't likely to mount them on .300 magnums, much less .458s. Scope manufacturers know the average buyer is a deer hunter who rarely shoots more than one 20-round box of ammo a year, or owns a rifle more powerful than the .30-06.

That approximate recoil level appears to be about the cutoff line for cheaper scopes. On rifles that kick like the .30-06 or 7mm Remington Magnum, even the least expensive scopes tend to hold up under twenty or thirty rounds a year, and are brighter than many of the "good" scopes of the 1960s. But stick the same scope on a .300 magnum of whatever variety, and bad things often happen. A .338 or .375 just speeds the bad things along.

But, you protest, even the cheapest scopes come with a guarantee. So what? Say 3 percent of a manufacturer's 3–9X scopes come back broken from the kick of .300 Weatherbys and .338 Winchesters. It's cheaper for the company to replace 3 percent of its scopes than to spend money on stronger construction and keener quality control.

If you hunt mostly from stands with a .25-06, 7mm-08, .270, or other relatively mild-kicking cartridge, then any scope will work, maybe forever. But if you plan to spend $4,000 and a couple of weeks of time on an elk hunt, you might consider a more reliable scope. So how do you find one?

First, talk to as many people as possible before buying, especially those who shoot a lot or hunt with rifles of .300 magnum or larger. Varmint hunters (especially prairie-dog shooters) and big-bore target shooters are particularly good sources, since their scopes have to put up with thousands of rounds.

Don't listen to the advice of most sporting-goods clerks, especially in big discount stores. They're out to sell whatever scope is overstocked, or the model with the biggest markup. One friend put three consecutive 3–9X cheapies—highly praised by the dink behind the local K-Mart counter—on his .300 Winchester before he gave up and asked for his money back.

Even clerks in genuine sporting-goods stores don't really know what they're talking about, especially those hired as extra help just before deer season starts. This, by the way, is a very bad time to buy a scope, despite all the preseason sales going on. If the scope isn't any good (and, as we shall see, a lemon can grow anywhere, even in a zillion-Deutsche-mark German factory), you won't have time to take care of the problem before the season starts.

Here I'll again cite the German DEVA tests. To test scope ruggedness, testers whacked the side of each scope with a 300-

gram (about one pound) rubber hammer five times. At least they hit the European scopes five times. Because American-style scopes feature a different reticle placement that the DEVA folks say is more likely to fail, these scopes (both American scopes and Pacific Rim scopes of American design) were whacked five additional times around the eyepiece.

(Let me see if I get this right: Because the American scopes were more likely to fail, they had to be hit twice as often? You figure it out. I can't.)

At any rate, after the scopes were given either five or ten "good" whacks, DEVA measured how much the reticle had shifted at 100 meters. This is what DEVA found:

Table 2.1

SCOPE	RETICLE SHIFT (in centimeters) *(horizontal/vertical)*
Bushnell 1.5–4.5X	1.8/4.0
Docter 1–4X24	0.0/0.0
Kahles 1.1–4.5X20	0.0/0.0
Leupold 1.5–5X20	0.0/0.5
Schmidt & Bender 1.25–4X20	0.0/0.0
Swarovski 1.5–4.5X20	0.0/0.5
Tasco 1.35–3.5X20	2.0/2.5
Zeiss 1.25–4X24	0.0/0.0

They also tested larger variables topping out at 10X to 12X:

Table 2.2

SCOPE	RETICLE SHIFT (in centimeters) *(horizontal/vertical)*
Docter 2.5–10X	0.0/0.0
Leupold 3.5–10X	2.4/0.8
Redfield 4–12X	3.1/1.4
Schmidt & Bender 3–12X	0.0/0.0
Swarovski 3–12X	0.0/0.0
Tasco 3–12X	0.0/0.0
Zeiss 2.5–10X	0.0/0.0

This is all very interesting, but I'd sure like to see what would happen if you whacked each of the European scopes another five times on the eyepiece—especially since they all feature an instant-focus eyepiece, which has to be more delicate than the American design.

One good rule of scoping hunting rifles is that the bigger the cartridge, the smaller the scope should be. There's no sense in mounting a 6–18X on a .375 anyway. But to repeat a point made above, the heavier a scope, the more likely it will eventually fall apart during recoil. This is one of the biggest problems with some of the new "tactical" scopes with range-estimation reticles such as the Sheperd and Nightforce.

These are becoming quite the rage among some long-range hunters, but I have had reliable reports of breakdowns after not very many shots with both scopes. The problems with such scopes arise in three ways: first, increased complexity, which tends to invoke Murphy's Law; second, sheer size and weight since these are big scopes; and third, most folks who want these scopes put them on hard-kicking rifles.

Before mounting, the scope should be dunked in warm water. Be forewarned that many "waterproof" scopes qualify only with the adjustment turret caps on. Oddly enough, these include the very cheapest scopes from the Pacific Rim and many of the finest European models. As far as I know, the only European scopes with O-rings in their adjustment turrets are a few Swarovski models and the Steiner and Leica lines made by Leupold.

The reason European manufacturers don't seal turrets lies in the different way European hunters view their gear. The typical German hunter, for instance, has a gunsmith mount and sight-in his scope. If he starts missing wild boar and red stag, he takes the thing back to his gunsmith to be "fixed," which a lot of the time means plain old sighting-in.

Much European hunting, too, takes place from stands or on drives. In wealthy European countries like Germany and Austria, a wild-boar drive is not the same as a Pennsylvania deer drive. Instead of you and your buddies taking turns blocking and driving, income-disadvantaged folks (known as peasants in less politically correct times) are hired to do the menial work of pushing game to the gun.

All of this results in an entirely different attitude toward rifles and scopes. On a tour of the Zeiss factory a few years ago, I pointed out that the company's scopes might fog if the owner took the turret caps off during damp weather. They looked at me curiously, and one official finally said, "But vy vould you effer take the caps off?" Because of this world view, I know at least one large Rocky Mountain sporting-goods store that flatly refuses to carry any European scopes; too many have come back fogged.

I personally use such European scopes fairly often, because they work fine for a lot of hunting. But if I planned on using any scope for wet-weather hunting—whether in

Gary Williams used his old .375 H&H Winchester Model 70 and a Leupold 1.75–6X variable to take this big Alaskan moose. A low-range, completely weatherproof variable is ideal for such hunting.

Louisiana, Alaska, or Maine—I'd for sure choose a model that's totally sealed.

But no matter whose scope you buy, dunk it to make sure it doesn't leak. Leave the turret caps on if you have doubts about your expensive European scope, but take the caps off all American and Japanese scopes. Warm water makes the gas inside the scope expand, forcing bubbles through any leaks.

Alas, many scopes emit more bubbles than Lawrence Welk from various parts of their anatomy. Be aware that some air can be trapped under the focus or power-change rings, but these bubbles stop after a few seconds. A real leak will continue for ten seconds or more. A leaker should be fixed or replaced.

The DEVA tests also included an underwater session. These must have been done with turret caps on, because several scopes that lack sealed adjustment turrets passed with flying colors. The scopes that leaked anyway were the 3–12X Tasco, the 2.5–10X Docter, and both Schmidt & Bender scopes, a 1.25–4X and a 3–12X. After dunking, each scope was also frozen for several hours—and all showed interior fogging in various degrees.

This has also been my experience. In talking about it with the Leupold representatives, they admitted that it's virtually impossible to totally eliminate all moisture from inside hunting scopes, even with nitrogen purging. Consequently, any scope will fog if first dunked in warm water, then frozen. So don't drop your rifle in a hot spring and then hike up a cold elk mountain. Reversing the sequence (first freezing, then dunking) doesn't have the same results, however.

Under virtually any hunting conditions, a scope that passes the dunk test without turret caps should remain fog-free—unless, of course, excess atmospheric moisture was sealed in at the factory. This can happen, which is why I also freeze my scopes, but begin with the scope at room tem-

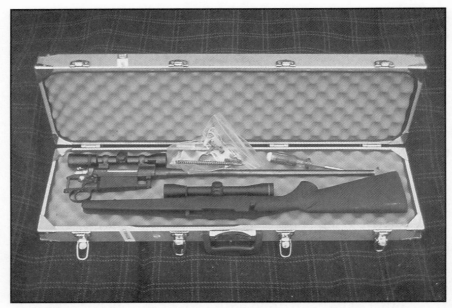

On trips into the deep outback a spare scope can come in handy. This is the author's takedown rifle case filled with his .338 FN Mauser, spare scope, and extra action parts.

perature, either long before or after dunking. If there's excess moisture trapped inside the scope, it will fog—usually on the inside of the ocular or objective lens—within an hour, even in a relatively warm refrigerator freezer. Frig freezers normally hold at 20–25 degrees Fahrenheit, versus zero or a little colder for chest freezers.

Once your new scope proves watertight, mount it on your rifle, shotgun, or handgun, and shoot it extensively as soon as possible. Twenty shots are OK on shotguns and big magnums, whether rifle or handgun, but forty work better on .30-06-class rifles and smaller handguns. A defective scope can be built in any factory, and twenty to forty shots often reveal any immediately loose parts.

Over the years a box or two of ammo has revealed factory defects not only in inexpensive scopes but also in scopes built by companies such as Bausch & Lomb, Leupold, and

Swarovski. Despite the most persnickety quality control, any company can put out a clunker.

Often scopes will work fine on light rifles but fall apart on bigger ones. I still have a 2–7X Compact Bausch & Lomb Scopechief that lived peaceably for several years on a Remington 700 chambered in .270 Winchester. Then I switched it to an Ultra Light Arms .300 Winchester Magnum weighing 6½ pounds. Within fifty shots, this super-accurate rifle was grouping three inches or more. Off to the factory it went, and has never bobbled since.

That should have taught me a lesson, but no. About that time, Swarovski sent me one of its 3–9X American models for testing. I put it on a lightweight Ruger 77 .30-06, where it performed fine on dim-light whitetails. Then the folks at Swarovski invited me to South Africa for some "field testing." Since I knew the hunt might involve some pretty large animals, I switched the 3–9X to my .375 H&H, bore-sighted the rig, and flew to Johannesburg.

At the ranch in the Transvaal I sighted-in. This .375 is very accurate, so it only took five shots to get it printing an inch high at one hundred yards. Then we went hunting. On the third day I shot a blesbok at two hundred yards, but despite a steady rest the bullet did not land exactly where I'd aimed. I shrugged it off, thinking perhaps the blesbok had taken a step just at the shot.

Then I shot at an impala ram at eighty yards, and hit the female standing next to him between the eye and the ear. "One of the most perfect meat shots I've ever seen!" my professional hunter said. "But I think we should check that bloody scope."

My super-accurate .375 was now grouping in a foot-long horizontal line. I'd take a shot, adjust the scope, and the next shot would be five inches in the opposite direction. Obviously something had gone screwy with the horizontal adjustment. I finished the hunt with the 4X scope the rifle usually wore—which I'd brought along, still in its mounts, as backup.

When I got back to the States, the Swarovski folks sent me another 3–9X, saying the bad one was from an early production run. They also sent along two boxes of factory .375 ammo. I shot that up, then tried my hand-loads, which clustered into a nice tight group. Nothing wrong with that scope. I have used any number of Swarovski scopes since on various hard kicking big-game rifles, and on varmint rifles that were shot hundreds of times in one day. None has ever bobbled.

The whole deal was not really Swarovski's fault; it was mine. I should have tested the scope on my .375 before I ever left Montana. Ever since, I have tested every scope with at least a box of shells before taking it anywhere—even if I've used it on a lighter-kicking rifle. Just this fall I switched a Leupold 6X42 from a custom Ruger #1 in 6.5x55 Mauser to an Ultra Light Arms Model 24 in .30-06. Federal's High Energy 180-grain loads chronograph over 2,900 feet per second from the 24-inch barrel of this 6-pound rifle, so it is really a very light .300 magnum. After twenty rounds the reticle broke, right where the bottom post joins the thinner section of the cross hair.

Yes, Leupolds carry an unconditional lifetime warranty, and, yes, it was fixed within ten days. But it could have broken during a hunt if I hadn't insisted on shooting a box of expensive ammo at the range rather than settling for merely sighting-in, which took only six shots.

Again, any scope can come out of the factory with a defect, and a box of ammo is cheap insurance against discovering any such defect right before an expensive hunt . . . or even hunts close to home. Say you get a crack at the whitetail buck of a lifetime ten miles from town, but your bargain scope is fogged. You only spent three bucks on gas, but how much is a big ten-point whitetail worth in hunting memories?

It might seem that steel-tubed scopes should be stronger than aluminum tubes. Well, no. Almost all the scopes sold these days are aluminum, and for several good reasons. Steel is much heavier than aluminum. If a steel tube is thinned down enough to make a lightweight scope, it has no noticeable strength advantage. I've proved this to myself by clamping junker scopes in a vise, then leaning on them until they bent. The light steel scopes (old Weavers) bent just as easily as newer aluminum scopes of the same weight.

So to gain any strength advantage, steel scopes must be much heavier. That in itself is a disadvantage, but let's say you're willing to haul an extra half-pound up the mountain if the scope is more rugged. Trouble is, steel thick enough to withstand the knocks and jars of hard hunting causes other problems. Bang the scope hard enough and the insides shake loose; instead of denting, the tough steel transmits shock to the lenses, reticle, and other delicate parts. Aluminum will dent with the same impact, but more often than not, the insides aren't affected and you can go on hunting. That is why 99 percent of the world's scopes now use aluminum tubes.

We are still waiting, by the way, for practical synthetic scope tubes. Bushnell introduced a 3–9X fiberglass-tubed scope a few years back, but the tube simply didn't have enough "hoop strength" and was too slick to hold in many rings. If you tightened the rings enough to hold the scope during recoil, the tube collapsed. Also, the synthetic tube expanded and contracted with temperature changes, playing hell with the lens mounts and seals.

Practical synthetic tubes are probably not too far off. Zeiss just brought out some wonderfully light binoculars using a high-impact plastic, and I suspect it won't be long before the technology is applied to scopes. When it does happen, scopes will be lighter, tougher, and probably less expensive.

The most usual scope problem on hard-kicking rifles is reticle-cell shift, which is also hardest to detect. This is what happened to that 2–7X Bausch & Lomb. You can easily tell when an adjustment spring breaks since the scope won't respond at all to any knob twirling. Loose lenses go clink in the night, and a snapped reticle becomes obvious the next time you aim the thing.

But when a reticle shifts, the common symptom is increasingly large groups. Once more, and with feeling—*Don't believe this can't happen with expensive scopes.* I've heard more about Zeiss scopes grouping weirdly than any other top brand, and I suspect the reason lies in the company's method of recoil testing. After each batch of Zeiss scopes comes off the assembly line, they're clamped into a recoil-tester in bunches of 100, then bashed 1,000 times lengthwise and 1,000 times up and down. Those that don't fall apart are deemed ready to sell.

As noted earlier, Leupold scopes have a reputation for toughness. At the Leupold factory testers pick a scope at random off the assembly line, then clamp that scope by its lonely self in a recoil-tester. The scope is then bashed over and over again with about the "kick" of a .375 H&H until it falls apart. Obviously, that scope is not sold to the public, but if it fails before Leupold's standards say it should, then that whole production run is pulled until the problem is found.

Now, remember the statement made at the beginning of this chapter: If you shoot any scope long enough, on any center-fire rifle, it will fall apart. Essentially, the recoil test from Zeiss results in its scopes having already been bashed 2,000 times before they're ever mounted on a rifle. That's why some Zeiss scopes don't last as long as some other brands, whether mounted on varmint rifles or .375s, despite their precise manufacture and quality materials.

In contrast, if the Leupold test indicates that there's no major screw-up in the assembly line during that run, the scopes are then sent out to the marketplace; therefore, new Leupold scopes sold in stores have not been pre-bashed. As we've seen, this doesn't absolutely guarantee that individual scopes are not defective, but it's a good indicator.

The foregoing may seem like I'm picking on Zeiss. Not at all. Zeiss optics, adjustments, and overall quality are second to none. But European shooting and hunting are very different from American shooting and hunting. Varmint shooting, for example, is almost unknown in Europe, especially the high-volume shooting done on prairie-dog towns. Since Europe doesn't have much game as large as our elk, moose, and big bears, you hardly ever see a European hunting rifle chambered for anything more powerful than the .30-06. And many Europeans simply do not hunt in driving rain or snow as often as we do, or sight-in their own rifles. Under those conditions, Zeiss scopes work wonderfully. But their design and testing can cause problems under American hunting conditions.

Similarly, some of Leupold's lesser priced fixed-power and Vari-X II scopes would not work nearly as well as a Zeiss for European night hunting, where bright optics matter more than anything else. So picking the very best scope for your style of hunting isn't as simple as buying only one brand. Too many factors are involved. In the next few chapters, we'll look at them.

EYE RELIEF AND FIELD OF VIEW

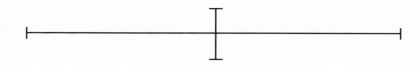

It's hard to decide where the other features of scope sights rate in overall importance, so I'll simply start with the back of the scope and work forward. It just so happens that a very important feature actually hangs in the air behind each scope. This feature is known as eye relief.

Eye relief, like Rodney Dangerfield, gets no respect. When we do talk about it, the conversation usually involves the long eye relief necessary when scoping handguns, Colonel Jeff Cooper's Scout rifles, and really hard kicking big bores. Though keeping a .460 Weatherby out of your eyeball is a worthy goal, eye relief can be just as important with light-kicking rifles because it directly affects field of view.

First, let's define our terms. Eye relief is the distance between your eye and the scope when the full field of view is visible. There are actually two eye reliefs: optical, the distance from the rear lens to your eye; and practical, the distance from the eyepiece (the rim around the lens) to your eye. Practical eye relief is the distance we're concerned with since that's what keeps a .460 at bay.

Most drawings of eye relief show a cone projecting from the rear lens, with the shooter's eye at the apex of the cone. But in reality the light coming from the rear of a scope resembles two cones connected at their points. Think of a small hourglass with the bottom placed against the scope's eyepiece, and you'll get the idea.

The waist of the hourglass forms the exit pupil, which was covered in chapter 1. As with the exit pupil, eye relief varies with scope magnification. Unfortunately, there's no simple way to calculate eye relief, but as a general trend,

Modern, high-combed rifles work very well with the 16- to 18-foot field of view of 6X scopes. The author (right) took this whitetail with a quick offhand shot with a Browning A-Bolt in 7mm Remington Magnum and a 6X Swarovski scope in river-bottom timber. On the left is Colorado outfitter Tom Tietz.

the cones of light coming from a high-magnification scope are shorter and steeper. The waist of the hourglass is also shorter and smaller in diameter; consequently, the eye must be placed more precisely in order to see the whole field of view. We call this critical eye relief.

Critical eye relief doesn't make much difference on a .223 used on prairie dogs at 300 yards, but it does when hunting big game, particularly at close range. If you ever get the chance to look through an old 2.5X Noske, one of the high-class scopes of the 1930s and 40s, you'll be amazed. Not only is the eye relief much longer than that of most modern scopes, but you can move your head back and forth two or three inches and still see the full field of view. The same effect can be seen in modern low-power handgun scopes and the scopes designed for Colonel Cooper's highly practical rifle. These modern scopes all have long, noncritical eye relief.

Latitude of eye relief is paid for, however, in field of view, which is obvious the first time you try to aim at a distant target with a handgun scope. With modern rifle scopes mounted directly above the action, or even a forward-mounted Scout scope, field of view is less critical, even though it is still often touted today, particularly in catalogs and advertising. A larger field supposedly allows us to find close targets faster, especially running game.

I first started doubting that an extra few feet of field was helpful for most hunting about twenty years ago, after a deer hunt in eastern Montana. My rifle was a Remington 700 BDL in .243 Winchester with a 6X Bushnell scope, an ideal combination for long shots in that open country. But all the experts said a 6X scope's field was way too small for running deer at close range.

On the second day of the hunt, I jumped a white-tailed buck from some wild rosebushes almost under my feet. The rifle came up, the scope found the deer, and the buck went

Big mule deer are thought of as long-range game, but this big Montana buck was taken while bedded under a spruce tree at much less than one hundred yards. Mid-range variable scopes provide both the field of view for close shots and the magnification for cross-coulee shooting.

down with a broken neck. I paced off the distance to where the buck fell—25 yards. He was even closer when I'd shot. Since then I've used 6X scopes (or variables set on 6X, which amounts to the same thing) not only to shoot other running deer but also to kill bull elk in lodgepole timber, all at ranges of 75 yards or less.

The reason so many early experts pushed the wide field of 2.5X or, at most, 4X scopes lay in crooked rifle stocks. In the 1930s hunting rifles were designed for iron sights, so their buttstocks were angled downward, allowing your eye to line up right along the barrel. Scopes were widely mistrusted in those days and, more often than not, were mounted high or to the side so the hunter could easily shift to irons when his dad-blasted optical sight fogged or broke. Combine a low buttstock with a high, off-center scope, and you need a field of view as wide as the Hudson River to find the Statue of Liberty, much less a running deer.

But today's rifles come with much straighter stocks designed for use with scopes, and today's trustworthy scopes can be mounted low and permanently. Modern 6X scopes have a field of at least 4½ feet at 25 yards, more than adequate for any deer or elk born this side of the Pleistocene Epoch. With a rifle stock designed to support the cheekbone directly behind the scope, a little practice makes short shots easy.

A few extra feet of field matters even less in very low-power scopes. A scope under 3X can (and should) be used with both eyes open, the cross hairs and ring of the eyepiece floating in a "field of view" as wide as your eyesight. This is the principle behind Jeff Cooper's forward mounted Scout scope, and it works. Your right eye looks through the scope while your left eye looks around it. Despite our modern-day fixation on high magnification, the system works equally well on grizzlies at 25 yards or deer at 250.

The field of view of a forward-mounted scope must be much smaller than that of a conventionally mounted scope. But at under 3X, it doesn't really matter if the scope's field is 22 feet at 100 yards (as with the Leupold Scout scope) or 44 feet (the field of the Bushnell 2.5X, an action-mounted model). You just keep both eyes open, place the reticle where you want it, and squeeze the trigger.

Long eye relief is one big reason the whole Leupold line is popular among users of big rifles. Leupolds consistently have longer eye relief than almost any other make, a recent exception being the Leica scopes—not so coincidentally made by Leupold. Four inches of eye relief is normal for Leupolds (except for their high-magnification variables—and even then it's there at the low end). Such long relief is also less critical, allowing quick aiming.

As you can see, the shorter the eye relief, the wider the field of view. I must say, however, that I sincerely doubt some of the numbers quoted in the following table (3.1). A few

Table 3.1

SCOPE	EYE RELIEF (inches)	FIELD OF VIEW (all fixed 6X) (feet at 100 yards)
Burris Fullfield	$3\frac{1}{2}-3\frac{3}{4}$	23
Redfield Tracker	$3\frac{1}{2}$	18
Schmidt & Bender	$3\frac{1}{4}$	21
Sightron	4	20
Steiner Penetrator	$3\frac{1}{10}$	$20\frac{2}{5}$
Swarovski	$3\frac{1}{2}$	23
Swift	$3\frac{3}{4}$	18
Tasco World Class	3	23
Weaver K6	$3\frac{3}{10}$	$18\frac{1}{2}$
Zeiss	$3\frac{1}{5}$	18

It's a simple job to design long eye relief into any scope—you simply sacrifice field of view. Despite some advertising, you can't have one without the other. According to the specifications in the 1998 Gun Digest, the Leupold M8 6X36 has a listed eye relief of $4\frac{3}{10}$ inches and a field of view of $17\frac{7}{10}$ feet. The eye-relief and field-of-view numbers of some other 6X scopes, taken from the same source, are given above.

manufacturers quote optical rather than practical eye relief—and the difference between the two can be half an inch or even more, depending on how far the lens is set into the eyepiece.

More often than you might guess, they simply lie. A decade ago I ordered a 4X scope from a well-known firm that shall remain nameless since they have since gone out of business. The advertised eye relief was four inches, which was great since I intended to mount it on a .338 Winchester Magnum. But when the scope arrived, it seemed a whole lot closer than that, especially since it bumped my eyebrow a couple of times during sighting-in.

So I decided to measure the eye relief. This wasn't simple, since it's damned hard to stick a ruler in your eye while holding it against the side of a scope. But the method I eventually came up with turned out to be much easier.

A fixed scope of not more than 4X or a variable of 2X to 3X at the low end is probably the best for true timber hunting.

First, lay the scope (or the rifle on which it's mounted) on a table. Place a ruler under the eyepiece of the scope, with the zero end even with the rear of the eyepiece. Then hold a small flashlight against the front lens of the scope and turn the flashlight on. Hold a piece of paper behind the scope, and move it back and forth along the ruler until you can see a sharply focused image of the flashlight's bulb. The distance between the eyepiece of the scope and the bulb's image is the optimum eye relief. (In a dark room, you can also hold the paper parallel to the rear of the scope and actually see the hourglass shape of the light. The waist of the hourglass is also the optimum eye relief.)

The result? My new 4X's eye relief measured just under three inches. I sent it back.

Do this with a few scopes, and a couple of things become obvious. One, as noted above, some catalogs lie, I'd guess because few customers measure eye relief. Two, eye relief varies with the magnification of most variable scopes. A 3–9X Nikon Monarch UCC sent to me for testing is pretty typical. At 3X eye relief measures 4½ inches; at 6X, 3¼ inches; and at 9X, 3 inches.

For much shooting this really isn't too bad a deal. Say you own a rifle chambered for a combination deer/varmint cartridge like the .257 Roberts. At 3X you've got long, flexible eye relief, just right for still-hunting the woods where many shots are taken offhand. When out on the prairie after pronghorn, you turn the scope up to 6X. In the wide open spaces you're far more likely to shoot from a sitting position, which tilts your head farther forward than the offhand position does. Losing an inch of eye relief actually helps you see the scope's full field of view. When shooting rock chucks or prairie dogs, you turn

EYE RELIEF AND FIELD OF VIEW

Eye relief is also a function of stock fit. This 1.5-5X Simmons has a lot of eye relief, but the rifle's stock is far too short for this 6-foot, 2-inch hunter.

the scope up to 9X where the short eye relief works fine for shooting from a prone position.

This is just ducky with a light-kicking rifle like a .257, or even a .270 or .280, but much more kick causes problems. This is where a lot of European scopes fail. Notice the short eye relief of the Schmidt & Bender, Steiner, and Zeiss (Table 3.1). In Europe, none of these will be mounted on anything more powerful than a .30-06, and European rifles are typically heavier than the "mountain" rifles commonly carried in America. Also, many European rifles are break-action single-shots, double rifles, or drillings, so their ammo isn't loaded to high velocities. Heavy rifles and modest ballistics result in milder recoil. On such rifles eye relief around three inches works fine.

But mount the same scopes on bigger guns and bad things happen. On a tour of the Zeiss factories in 1993, several gun writers got a chance to shoot running boar targets with a Remington 700 in 7mm Magnum, mounted with a 3–9X Zeiss. Several of us got bumped, albeit lightly, by the rubber ring around the eyepiece.

Then we shot an A-Square rifle (the Hannibal, I believe) chambered in .416 Rigby. This came mounted with a 1.25–4X scope, supposedly to demonstrate how tough Zeiss scopes really are. I don't know if anything was proved there, since all told the whole group shot the .416 maybe ten times. Some refused to shoot it at all because the first couple of shooters got whacked—not bumped—by the scope. One guy, I guess to prove his manhood, shot

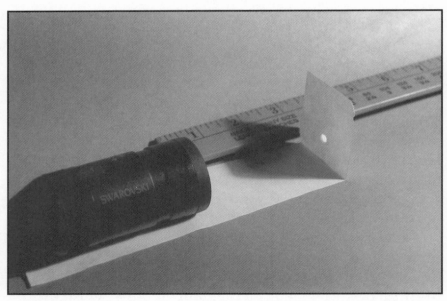

Eye relief can be measured with a small flashlight, ruler, and piece of paper. The figures of many manufacturers are incorrect or incomplete; the eye relief of most variable scopes shortens as magnification goes up.

the damned thing two or three times, the predictable result being a big, juicy bruise above his right eye.

Because of their short eye relief, many European
scopes feature a collapsible, spring-loaded eyepiece
rimmed by heavy rubber. Such an eyepiece won't cut your
eyebrow; instead, as the late Wyoming gun writer Bob
Milek pointed out, "It just bludgeons you to death!" To
take care of the occasional brow-bump caused by shots
from odd positions, many American and Japanese scopes
feature a light rubber ring around the eyepiece. The exception is Leupold, whose scopes are made of bare
aluminum; you don't need a rubber rim if eye relief is long
enough. (The German DEVA report on hunting scopes criti-
cizes Leupold for not using rubber on its eyepieces. The
Germans simply don't get eye relief at all.)

Aside from the Leupold-made Leicas (a sort of hy-
brid European/American design), Swarovskis are the
only European scopes with eye relief long enough for
hard-kicking rifles. But even the Swarovski folks tend
to get things a little backward. One of their ad guys recently showed me a new 3–10X, crowing that the field
of view was "two feet wider than Leupold's 3.5–10X!"
Well, yeah—and Leupold's eye relief is longer. Field of
view or eye relief? It always comes down to that simple
trade-off. If Leupold wanted a wider field, it would stick
one in there.

Recently, I've also noticed a trend toward shorter
eye relief in American and Japanese scopes. Bausch &
Lomb was for a long time closest to Leupold in eye relief. I have a couple of the old Bal-series scopes around.
The 4X Balfor has an eye relief of almost 4 inches, while
a 1.5–6X Balvar has 4½ inches of eye relief at 1.5X, and
over 3 inches at the higher powers.

Bausch & Lomb's latest Elite series, however, shows a definite trend toward more field and shorter eye relief. The longest eye relief of any B&L scope listed today is 3³⁄₁₀ inches, on its lowest-power model, the 1.5–4.5X Elite 3000. This would work OK, though it's a little marginal for the hard kickers—.375s, .416s, and .458s—that such a power range fits so neatly.

But the eye relief of my own sample scope measures a very short 2½ inches at every magnification. I started wondering about this after mounting the scope on my Ultra Light Arms .30-06 and sighting-in with some of Federal's 180-grain High Energy loads. My eyebrow got bumped more than once, so I measured the eye relief. There's no way I'd ever mount such a scope on a .338, much less a .416.

Today I sat down and measured the eye relief of every scope in the house. (A few were missing because their rifles were off at various gunsmiths.) You'll note in Table 3.2 that the eye relief of that 1.5–4.5X Bausch & Lomb didn't change at all through the whole magnification range. I suspect that's due to new engineering developed for handgun scopes. Handgun shooters, too, have always wanted variable scopes, but until recently these were always plagued by wide swings in eye relief. Shooters found that while a certain scope might work just right at 2X on their .44 Magnum, allowing the arm's-length hold desirable for hard kickers, they often had to hold the gun with elbow bent to see through the same scope at 4X.

But scope makers eventually licked that problem, and the same engineering seems to have been applied to some rifle scopes as well. When I measured the eye relief of the variable scopes in my collection, some changed much more than others. Here's the chart:

Table 3.2 Eye relief in inches at:

SCOPE	1X	1.5X	2X	3X	4X	6X	7X	9X	10X
1–3X Weaver	5			3					
1–4X Leupold	4¼			4	3½				
1–5–4.5X B&L 3000	2½ at all magnifications								
1.5–6X Balvar		4½		3½		3⅕			
2–7X B&L 3000			5¼		3½		3		
2–7X Redfield			3½			3⅖	3¼		
3–9X Leupold				4⅖		3¾		3½	
3–9X Nikon				4½		3¼		3	
3–9X Zeiss				4		3¼		3$\frac{1}{10}$	
3.5–10X Leupold				4		3¾			3⅖
3–10X Swarovski	3⅖ at all magnifications								
2–10X Weaver			3			2¾			2½
2.5–10X Tasco			3½			3½			3
3–11X Pentax	3 at all magnifications								
4–12X B&L 3000	2½ at all magnifications								

It seems that a few scope makers have licked the "problem" of eye-relief changes at varying magnifications, some entirely and others to a lesser extent. Also, some scopes vary considerably from the manufacturer's specifications, though you couldn't really say any manufacturer lies all the way across the board. Some scopes in certain lines matched right up with the catalog, while others didn't. But too many manufacturers state only one eye relief, very often the longest.

I also measured some fixed-power scopes. Here there were no major-league surprises. Most modern 4X scopes showed nice long eye relief of 3½ to 4 inches, while 6X scopes varied more, from a low of 3 inches for a Swarovski 6X36 to a long 4½ inches for the Leupold 6X42. A couple of ancient 2X scopes from my collection—a 330 Weaver and a Lyman Alaskan—both have eye relief of at least 4 inches.

It seems that eye relief keeps shrinking. Don't get me wrong; 3 inches is a good minimum for rifles chambered for all-round American game cartridges such as the .270 Winchester, 7mm Remington Magnum, and .30-06 Springfield. But on a .300 magnum of whatever brand, or a .338 Winchester, I'd be happier with 3½ inches. That's a bare minimum for rifles from .375 on up, and 4 inches is better.

Admittedly, though, a lot of this really depends on the shooter. I'm not a stock "crawler," always inching up on my scope, so unless eye relief is well under three inches, I rarely have a problem. But my friend Bill McRae is so bad I suspect he might acquire a "magnum eyebrow" from a Scout scope! If you get bumped or cut too frequently, look to longer eye relief for help—and mount that scope as far forward as possible.

For instance, there's really little difference between the eye relief of the 3–9X Nikon and Leupold scopes listed—

but with both scopes on 9X, the extra half-inch of the Leupold might help a lot on something like a .300 Weatherby. On a whitetail rifle chambered for a milder cartridge such as the 7mm-08 or .270, I'd probably go with the Nikon, simply because its optics are significantly brighter. In most whitetail hunting situations, you need all the brightness you can get.

In handgun scopes, many experienced shooters still like fixed, low-power models. The reason lies in long, non-critical eye relief. Bausch & Lomb's 2X is a fine example, with a listed eye relief of anywhere from 9 to 26 inches. Now, that is flexible! But low-power handgun scopes, and even the Scout scopes, suffer from low twilight factor, that constant malady of low magnification. Even with handgun scopes, 4X works much better in low light—the reason more and more handgun hunters use variables. If the light's good enough at 2X, fine, but if not, 4X works much better.

One last note on field of view. Field of view can also be increased with the use of a bigger ocular lens, exactly what some of the Europeans and even a few American/Japanese scopes use. Trouble is, on bolt-action rifles (and even some others), the scope must be mounted higher to clear the larger eyepiece. This forces the shooter to lift his head off the stock, in turn making it a little harder to find the full field of view.

Redfield made an interesting variation of this approach in the TV-screen view of its Widefield. This increases the field of view horizontally (in theory, I guess, to help in shooting running game), while not requiring the higher mounts of big round eyepieces. For a brief time a few other manufacturers made such scopes, but for years before its demise Redfield had the market all to itself. I suspect Widefields didn't sell all that well, though I do know one hunter who swears by them.

The trouble with all these manipulations is that an extra few feet of field at one hundred yards doesn't make a bit of difference. But advertising aimed at the inexperienced hunter, claiming a wide field as the main secret to hunting success, will always con a few customers. Despite those claims, anyone used to handling a modern rifle can find a deer just as easily with a twenty-foot field of view as with a thirty- or forty-foot field.

FOCUS, RETICLES, AND PARALLAX

It continually amazes me how many shooters aren't aware that they should focus their rifle's scope. It's done by turning the eyepiece of the scope, though the engineering varies between American- and European-style scopes.

American-style scopes feature an eyepiece (the rear bell of the scope, which includes the ocular lens) threaded onto the scope tube and held in place by a lock ring. To focus, loosen the lock ring, then turn the eyepiece in or out until the reticle is sharply focused.

European-style scopes focus by turning the rear rim of the eyepiece. The eyepiece itself remains stationary, while the ocular lens cams in and out. In fine thread American-style focusing you may have to turn the eyepiece a few dozen times, but one turn of a European-style scope provides a wide range of focus. Since the ocular lens isn't locked in place, the scope can instantly be focused for different shooters.

Photos above and below represent long-range varmint rifles. Long-range varmint shooters typically use scopes of over 10X, which require adjustable objective lenses.

Also, older eyes can't adjust to varying ranges as well as young eyes can. My friend Sil Strung found in her mid-fifties that her eyes simply wouldn't accommodate the set focus of the 4X Leupold on her .270. I mounted a Bushnell Trophy 4X scope on the rifle, since the Trophys feature a European style focus ring. It worked fine; she could instantly change focus, whether hunting whitetails from tree stands or pronghorns in eastern Montana. (Those new Bushnells, by the way, are one reason I use the terms American-style and European-style to describe the two focusing systems. Several American and Japanese scopes use the European system these days, and several Swarovski models feature the American system.)

One secret for focusing American-style scopes: Do it at dusk. During midday the pupils of our eyes shrink to very small dots. If you're even a semi-serious photographer, you know that closing down the *f-stop* on a camera lens results in much greater depth of field. The same effect occurs with our eyes. You can focus a scope at noon on a sunny day, then find the scope not so sharp during the dim light of early morning and late evening. By adjusting the scope at dusk, when your eyes have their shallowest depth of field, you'll focus the scope more precisely.

So why do some scopes also feature objective lenses that turn in and out as well? Called, naturally enough, adjustable objectives, these lenses help focus high-magnification scopes, but their main purpose lies in correcting parallax.

To most hunters, parallax is an even less exciting subject than eye relief, but its effects are far more important to accuracy. One dictionary defines parallax as "the apparent displacement of an observed object due to the difference between two points of view." In shooting terms, this means the target *moves* when the shooter's eye shifts behind the scope.

You can demonstrate a simple form of parallax by forming a circle with your forefinger and thumb and holding that hand at arm's length. Next, close one eye and aim that circle at a light switch across the room. Holding your hand steady, move your head back and forth. The light switch will move inside the circle. That's parallax.

The same thing occurs in a rifle scope. Here I'll have to be a little technical, but I will try to make things as painless as possible since tech-talk hurts me even more than it does you.

A rifle scope is a simple telescope, a series of lenses within a tube. There are no prisms, mirrors, or other fancy stuff, just one lens sending light on to the next until the light gets shoved out the rear of the scope and into your eye.

All rifle scopes must have at least three lenses. Two we've talked about already, the objective lens at the front of the scope and the ocular lens at the rear. Actually, these two lenses would work by themselves, if we could accept an upside-down world.

We see this same effect with a magnifying glass. A magnifying glass is a convex lens, just like a scope's objective, which means that it is thicker in the middle than at the edges. Held close to an object, it magnifies, but hold it farther away and people appear to walk on ceilings.

The same thing happens with the objective lens of a scope. If we had just two lenses, the objective would project an upside-down, backward image on the ocular lens. So simple telescopes use a middle lens, called the erector lens, to turn the image right-side up. In showing the image to our eye, the ocular lens at the rear of the scope functions much like a movie screen.

Remember the cones of light formed at the rear of the scope? The same thing happens inside the scope. Here there are two hourglasses, one between the objective and the erector lens, and one between the erector and the ocular lens.

For a scope to help us aim, we need a reticle in there somewhere. Otherwise we'd just be pointing an empty telescope at a deer and hoping the bullet landed where we were looking. There are only two places to put a reticle and have it remain in focus—on the *waists* of the two hourglasses. These are called focal planes, where any object inside the scope will be in focus.

Here's where things get tricky. There is no exact spot to place the reticle because the right spot varies with range. Think again of the circle made with your finger and thumb. If you hold your hand three inches from the light switch, there's almost no parallax; the switch doesn't move as you shift your head. But back your hand up a foot and the light switch definitely moves with any head-shift. The same thing happens in any riflescope when the reticle isn't in the "sweet spot."

This effect increases with magnification. For all practical purposes, parallax doesn't exist in the 4X or 6X scopes used for big-game hunting. Here the reticle is placed to eliminate parallax at 150 to 200 yards; at shorter or longer ranges it amounts to less than an inch. This scarcely matters on the body of a deer. Even in variables up to 10X, parallax isn't a major factor since 8X and 10X scopes are used at longer ranges. Eliminate parallax at 250 yards and you're fine at any range up to a quarter-mile or more.

But higher magnification can cause real problems, especially in big variables. Variables change magnification by shifting the erector lens. They're mounted in a slotted tube that cams back and forth as we turn the magnification ring.

With lower-power variables from 1–4X to 2–7X this isn't a problem. But once we arrive at the popular 3–10X range, things get difficult. Here any scope engineer must make compromises. Most manufacturers try to minimize parallax at the higher settings, figuring a couple of inches won't be noticed at 3X or 4X.

But some don't. A couple of years ago Pentax sent me one of its 2–8X Lightseekers. After it passed the warm-

Most hunters think of .22 rimfires as short-range rifles, but given a good variable scope with an adjustable objective lens, modern .22s can be used out to 200 yards or even more.

water dunk test, I mounted it on a very accurate Ruger #1 in 7x57 and went to the range. Setting the scope on 4X, I shot two or three times at 30 yards to get on paper before shooting at 100 yards.

It was weird. This rifle normally groups three shots of its favorite handload into less than ³/₄ inch, but the first group went almost 3 inches. Well, maybe the bore needed to be fouled before it would settle down. I let the rifle cool while I tested a couple of others, then I shot it again. This group was "better"—slightly over 2 inches!

I tested all the scope-mount screws. They were tight. Finally, I set the rifle on the sandbags and moved my head back and forth. The reticle moved about 4 inches across the target! Maybe, I thought, it's correct for 250 yards or some other distant range. Nope. Doing the same test at 200 and 300 yards showed even more reticle movement.

So I called my friends at Pentax, and they shipped another 2–8X. When it arrived a couple of days later, I mounted it on the same rifle, set the scope on 4X, and checked the parallax. This scope was better—maybe 3 inches at 100 yards—but still way too much.

So I called Pentax again. They suggested I check the parallax at 2X and 8X. Bingo! No parallax! But to me, a big game variable is most useful at middle magnifications, say 3X to 6X, and the scope showed anywhere from 2 to 4 inches of parallax at those settings. Pentax chooses to eliminate parallax at both ends of the spectrum.

I may be nuts, but this doesn't seem right to me. In contrast, a Leupold 3–9X Vari-X II shows maybe 3 inches of parallax at any setting—at 400 yards. A 3–9X Nikon, 2.5–10X Bausch & Lomb, 3–10X Swarovski, and 3.5–10X Leupold Vari-X III show even less. In fact, parallax is almost unnoticeable at all settings.

Aside from being designed into the scope, parallax can also show up later. As touched on in the last chapter, any shift in the reticle causes parallax. Most reticles are mounted in a ring of metal called the reticle cell that's pinned, screwed, glued, or otherwise attached inside the scope tube. Sometimes they come loose—but usually they don't come totally unmoored. Instead, the reticle cell shifts forward a fraction of an inch, creating brand-new parallax.

This has happened to so many scopes I've tested that I've lost count, and I'd have to rate it the most common failure in any scope, no matter the quality. So anytime I receive a new scope that's supposed to be not only incredibly "affordable" but also guaranteed tough enough to take the recoil of big magnums, I grow instantly suspicious and mount the thing on my lightweight .338. Twenty rounds usually separate advertising from truth.

The most common symptom is larger groups, often strung up and down. Such "stringing" causes most shooters to look for other problems, especially poor stock bedding, when the scope is the real cause. The stock of our rifle, resting against our cheek, tends to keep our head centered horizontally behind the scope. But any up-or-down head movement causes vertical fliers.

Scopes may also come from the factory with bad parallax. For the best results, final reticle settings should be made after the objective lens is mounted. One 1.5–5X Simmons Whitetail evidently didn't have the objective screwed down tightly when the reticle was mounted. How did I know? Well, for one thing the objective housing was loose, right out of the box. When I tightened it, parallax amounted to nearly 6 inches at 100 yards. When I backed the objective out again, parallax went away. So whoever set the reticle at the factory never noticed that the objective was unscrewed several threads. One Burris 6X had such bad parallax that a custom .280 that normally grouped three 139-grain Hornadys into half an inch, scattered shots into 4 or 5 inches. But the scope's replacement did just fine.

So I always check parallax on new scopes. The obvious way to do it is at the range, by sandbagging the rifle and shifting your head back and forth. But parallax also shows up on collimators [a fixed telescope used to accurately adjust the line of sight]. If you have your scope mounted at the store where it's purchased, ask the folks there to let you look through the scope while the collimator is still stuck in the muzzle. Shift your head back and forth. If the reticle slides across the collimator grid more than an inch, you need another scope.

There are two main systems for eyepiece focusing, the European quick-focus style and the American lock-ring style. The word "style" is important here because there's some crossover these days. The Pentax 3–11X at top uses an American lock-ring, as does the Swarovski 3–10X (third from top) while the Leupold 3.5–14X LPS (second from top) and Zeiss 2–10X (bottom) feature the European quick-focus.

The grid on my Bushnell collimator is marked off in what are supposed to equal 4-inch squares at 100 yards. Because of varying barrel lengths on rifles, this is only an approximation, but a very close one. If a reticle shifts across more than a quarter of one of those squares, I know the scope has parallax problems.

Scopes of more than 10X absolutely require some mechanical means of correcting parallax. Since parallax is controlled by the distance between the objective lens and the reticle, there are two ways to do this. Most scopes use an objective lens that screws in and out, but some feature a reticle that can be shifted back and forth.

The turret housing of many older scopes was attached to the reticle. The housing could be loosened by turning a couple of screws, allowing the housing to slide back and forth along the scope tube for a short distance, adjusting parallax. That system didn't help waterproofing, however.

There are disadvantages to adjustable objectives. They're a little more delicate than a fixed objective, and many use an extra lens, decreasing light transmission slightly. It's also hard to adjust the thing while aiming the scope, so some newer scopes feature a reticle adjustment on the side of the tube. All those I've seen have been the new "tactical" scopes, designed for use by military and police, but it's not a bad idea for varmint shooting.

Parallax can also help explain the occasional rifle that shoots better at longer ranges than at 100 yards. The most common explanation is that some bullets don't fully stabilize until well past 100 yards. But after many experiences with various scopes, I suspect some scopes simply have significant parallax at 100 yards, which disappears at 200 or 300 yards.

Adjustable-objective scopes can turn many ordinary .22 rifles into tack drivers. Most .22 scopes are set to be parallax-free at short ranges of 50 or 75 yards, but that virtually guarantees they'll show parallax at any other range—and in a .22 used for head-shooting squirrels a little parallax goes a long way. My own super-accurate Remington .22 features a 4–12X Bausch & Lomb Elite 3000, which not only allows me to see very small targets but also eliminates parallax at any range from 25 yards out.

Parallax, unlike good, cheap, elk outfitters, does exist.

VARIABLE
SCOPES

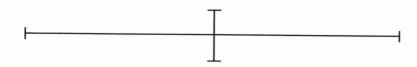

Back when most of the hunters I knew used "primitive" weapons like 1903 Springfields and 4X scopes, the variable riflescope was just starting to be accepted. This was in the mid-1960s. Most shooters still think of variables as a "modern" development even though Zeiss (who else?) first began marketing practical riflescopes that would change magnification back in the 1930s.

These first variables were delicate and complex, and featured what is called a first-focal-plane reticle. The first-plane reticle supposedly has one virtue and one vice. When the magnification in first-plane scopes changes, the point of impact never shifts—but the size of the reticle in relationship to the target also never changes. This may not sound like too big of a deal, but in big-game hunting a cross hair that looks just right at 5X looks like rope at 10X, or shrinks to fine blond hair at 2X.

Even in the early days of variables, optical engineers knew a solution to this problem, but first-plane reticles were used for decades because the solution didn't work with the manufacturing methods of the time. To understand the solution, we need to understand how a variable scope works.

In a fixed-magnification scope the erector lenses are held inside a stationary tube. In variable scopes this tube slides back and forth, cammed by the turning of a ring on the outside of the scope. The reticle can be placed in two locations: between the objective (front) lens of the scope and the power-change tube, or between the power-change tube and the ocular (rear) lens.

When in the first focal plane (in front of the power-changing mechanism), the reticle is magnified along with the image, and its size and position relative to the target don't change. When the reticle is placed in the second focal plane, behind the power-changing mechanism, its apparent size stays the same—but point of impact can shift if the power-change tube doesn't slide precisely back and forth along the same axis in the center of the scope.

Early on, making a second-plane scope work precisely would have involved careful hand-fitting of each scope, and so was simply too expensive for mass manufacture. To cope with the growing and shrinking first-plane reticle, most European scopes featured a set of three or four heavy posts converging on a fine, center cross hair, while America's Bausch & Lomb scopes used a finely tapered reticle actually etched on glass.

European hunters prefer first-plane reticles. They hunt a lot at night, when the better twilight factor of higher magnification is an advantage. When they turn their scopes up, the reticles look heavier, a real advantage when aiming at a wild boar in a moonlit meadow.

But Americans saw variables not as aids to night aiming but as all-round scopes. With a twist of the wrist a 3–9X scope would be perfect for everything from elk in the timber to long-range varmints. Consequently, American hunters wanted a

Modern hunters prefer variable-power scopes. Quality variables are rugged and reliable, and can be found in a size to fit all requirements. These two rifles are on a South African safari. The wooden-stocked .375 Mauser made by Holland & Holland is mated with a 1.5–5X Leupold, while the synthetic-stocked Mark X Mauser .30-06 uses a 3–9X Swarovski.

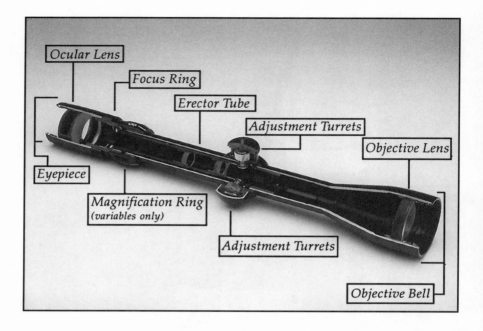

Ocular Lens

Focus Ring

Erector Tube

Adjustment Turrets

Objective Lens

Eyepiece

Magnification Ring
(variables only)

Adjustment Turrets

Objective Bell

reticle that could quadrisect a woodchuck's head at 9X but stand out plainly in dim woods at 3X.

So American manufacturers started working with second-plane scopes until they got it right. Redfield, I believe, was the first to solve the problem back in the late 1950s—the reason variable scopes suddenly became popular in the 1960s. But in the last twenty years, computer-driven machinery has made second-plane variables essentially foolproof, even in relatively inexpensive scopes.

So why do some American hunters buy first-focal-plane scopes? It turns out first-plane scopes have one other virtue: The reticle's constant size in relationship to the target makes using the reticle as a rangefinder much easier. More hunters are hunting white-tailed deer than ever before and under conditions that make first focal-plane scopes advantageous. Under the intense pressure of longer seasons and more hunters (just take a look at any magazine rack and count the deer-hunting titles), whitetails have become by far the most nocturnal big-game animal on this continent.

Modern deer hunters realize that more magnification helps them see better during those twilight hours when deer move, but at high magnification many second-plane reticles disappear shortly after sunset while first-plane reticles grow more visible. Essentially, we're finding that our European cousins knew something useful about variable scopes all along.

Despite all that, the second-plane scope remains the top choice among American hunters, something recognized even by the more intelligent European manufacturers, which usually market a line of special "American-style" scopes with 1-inch tubes and second-plane reticles. The reason they do this is that most American hunters still see variable scopes as multipurpose instruments or, these days, as extremely precise long-range aiming devices in which a finer reticle works better.

Thirty years ago many gun writers thought variables inferior to fixed-power scopes. Variables were heavier, fell apart easily, changed point of impact, and, because of the compromises inherent in moving lenses, were optically inferior. You still see these charges made from time to time.

These days it's rare to find even the cheapest bubble-pack 3–9X showing any significant change of impact. Though in the very cheapest scopes a fixed-power might be more rugged, many manufacturers produce inexpensive variables specifically for shotgun use. After all, a light slug gun's recoil is tougher than any rifle short of a .375 H&H. The first variables needed to be extra long and heavy, which helps in keeping the view sharp through big changes in magnification. But back then we didn't have the marvelous optical glass we have today, or computerized design programs. These days you can buy a 3–10X scope that's only a couple of ounces heavier than the typical 4X scope of the 1950s, and the smaller variables can be even lighter than those old 4Xs.

They're also brighter. Though the very finest fixed-power scopes are still slightly brighter than the best variables (a by-product of the fewer lenses in fixed-power systems), the difference is very slight and is offset by the higher twilight factor of big variables. Sure, a fixed 6X will be slightly brighter than a 3–10X variable of the same make set at 6X. But crank the 3–10X up and you'll be able to see more under all but the darkest conditions. In North America real darkness occurs after legal shooting hours.

In practical terms, because most scope manufacturers sell far more variable scopes than fixed-powers, variable optics tend to be better. In Leupold's line, for instance, all but one of the fixed scopes feature single-coated lenses and simply aren't as bright as its multi-coated Vari-X III line. The other day I compared a plain old 4X Leupold with a 1.5–5X Vari-X III.

In theory the 4X should be brighter. It's got a bigger 28mm objective versus the 20mm of the 1.5–5X, providing an 8mm exit pupil—far larger than the 1.5–5X's 4mm exit pupil. It also has fewer lenses than the variable, cutting down on light loss on each lens surface. Because of multi-coating, the little variable is just as bright, if not brighter, and provides a much clearer view when looking toward the sun. Both scopes weigh about the same, a little more than nine ounces, though the variable is slightly trimmer.

Despite all that, you can run into occasional problems with variable scopes. Most can be prevented by three simple tests. First, turn the magnification ring. It should not turn easily, and the rings on better scopes turn harder. There's a simple reason for this: a tighter fit of all moving parts. This is desirable in variable scopes since any slop in the erector tube can mean a shift in point of impact. If you don't believe me, go down to your nearest sporting-goods store sometime and fiddle with as many scopes as they'll tolerate. Scopes with names like Bausch & Lomb, Leupold, Pentax, Swarovski, and Zeiss will require noticeably more effort to change magnification than most Bushnell, Simmons, and Tasco models.

You may have to buy the scope for the next two tests, but if the scope fails either, the manufacturer should replace it. First, mount the scope and place the rifle in a vise so that the reticle rests on some object 100–200 yards away, or slip a collimator into the muzzle. Then look through the scope and turn the magnification ring. The reticle should remain on the same aiming point, either across the street or on the collimator grid, through the scope's entire range of magnification. If there's any shift, the scope's defective and the manufacturer should replace it. (It also might behoove you to perform the same test while turning a big scope's adjustable objective. Once in a while you'll find a reticle shift there, too. This is caused by the lens being cockeyed.)

Last comes the dunk test, as described in the chapter on reliability. Variables do have an extra hole through their body, the slot cut for the camming stud on the magnification ring. In theory this leaves more chance for water to get inside the scope. I've never had it happen on a quality scope, but why not make sure?

What should impress you after you've performed these tests on several scopes is how rarely modern variables show any significant reticle shift or leak around the power ring. In all the testing I've done in the past half-dozen years, I have found only one scope with any significant reticle shift, and have never found one that leaked around the power ring. During that time I've tested at least one hundred variable scopes.

The only real problem I've seen with modern variables was touched on in chapter 2, and might be termed inappropriate use. This comes from mounting too big a scope on too powerful a rifle. Big variables (from 4–12X up) tend to unravel, particularly in the erector tubes, if you insist on mounting them on hard-kicking big-game rifles from .300 magnum on up. This is becoming more and more the style, however, as some hunters seemed determined to shoot at any animal they can possibly see.

Personally, I have no real use for a .30-378 or a big-game scope topping out at more than 10X, but if you do, then buy the very best scope you can. Even then, try to find the lightest scope available. Extra weight means extra inertia when the big gun recoils.

If you buy good scopes and make them smaller as the guns get bigger, you'll rarely have a problem. Most of the problems I see and hear of occur with .300 magnums of all sizes and scopes larger than the popular 3–10X. Above .30 caliber most hunters seem content with smaller variables, perhaps because .338s, .375s, and .416s are usually used on larger animals, while many .300 magnum shooters are after the ultimate long-range pronghorn, sheep, and deer rifle.

But those breakdowns are rare occurrences, caused by pushing the rifle/scope package to the limit. For most hunters, modern variables are even more reliable, in every way, than the 4X scopes our fathers and grandfathers used.

All that said, why would anyone choose a fixed-power scope? I do myself, and often. About a third of my rifles have fixed scopes of 2.5X to 6X. Often it's matter of style. A fixed 4X just looks right on certain classic rifles, such as a Ruger #1 in 7x57 Mauser. Fixed scopes also cost less, and for most big-game hunting, we really don't give up any practical advantage when using a 4X or 6X.

There's also something esthetically pleasing about simplicity, especially in a world that seems to grow more complex with each sunrise. Fifty years ago, a 4X scope on your .30-06 would have put you on the cutting edge of long-range accuracy. Today the same scope and rifle mark you as a reactionary, either hopelessly behind the times or a hunter who insists on getting close enough to make sure. I guess this is all part of what was termed situational ethics back in the 1960s. Whatever side you prefer, don't worry about the scope. These days there's one out there for you.

RETICLES

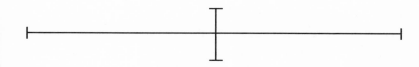

Like windshield wipers, we hardly ever think about scope reticles unless we can't see or they fall apart. Up through the 1960s, arguments raged in the pages of the sporting magazines over the merits of fine cross hairs, thick cross hairs, dots, and posts. The introduction of Leupold's Duplex a couple of decades ago put a stop to that, since everybody else copied it. Now it's hard to find a scope without a thick-and-thin aiming point. They can still be had, usually by special order only, but they find favor mostly among target shooters, not hunters.

Originally, many scope reticles were made of natural fibers such as human hair and spider webs. These proved satisfactory for the standard cross hairs and were used in many scopes even long past World War II. Most post-and-dot reticles were added to fine cross hairs. The post was usually an actual metal piece mounted in front of the cross hairs, but the dot could be simply a dot of glue dabbed where the hairs crossed.

One reticle I've never figured out was the variable dot my old hunting buddy Ben Burshia had in his pre-World

War I Bausch & Lomb. This was a very ancient scope, purchased when Ben bought his .30-06 Winchester Model 70 in 1936, the very first year Model 70s were made. The scope was a standard prewar B&L of about 2X, without internal adjustments, in the adjustable B&L mount. When you twisted a ring (much like the magnification ring on modern variables), the dot shrank or swelled. Mostly Ben left the dot small, except in dim light.

When I first saw the scope in the early 1970s, I assumed the variable dot was a standard feature with B&L scopes. Since then I've gotten to know the folks at B&L pretty well, and they can't find any record of such an option in their old catalogs. It must have been an aftermarket custom installation, and nobody I've talked to has ever heard of such a thing. Ben traded the rifle off a few years later, when I wasn't looking, for a brand-new Savage 99 in .243 Winchester, com-

The modern four-post and cross-hair reticle can be used as a very effective rangefinder. The small paper dot on the adjustment housing of this 6X Swarovski shows the number of inches between the cross hairs and the top of the bottom post at 100 yards.

plete with impressed checkering and a 3–9X Tasco. Otherwise, I'd have it now and could perhaps solve the mystery.

For decades cross hairs remained the essential American hunting reticle, and natural fibers worked just fine, due to reasons that still relate to modern reticles. They were light and flexible, which are generally good things, since a heavy reticle tends to shift or even snap, especially when someone drops a rifle or a .416 goes off.

As technology progressed, most scope makers switched to fine wire. In some ways wire was not quite so satisfactory as hair or spider webbing. When I was sixteen, two older (and larger) friends were carrying the halves of a deer out of a deep and snowy canyon in the Absaroka Mountains while I carried our three rifles. I slipped on a snow-covered boulder, and one buddy's rifle slipped from my shoulder. The 4X Weaver hit the boulder, and the horizontal cross hair snapped. It cost five bucks to fix, a lot of money to a sixteen-year-old in 1968.

Other misfortunes happen to reticles. One summer I got a phone call from David Miller, the famed Arizona rifle maker. He'd had a couple of custom horizontal cross hairs installed in the Leupold scope atop the .300 Weatherby Magnum he used for long-range Coues deer shooting. His theory (a good one) was that two cross wires would allow him to estimate range more accurately than with a simple Duplex.

Miller was out on a hot day doing some off-season varmint shooting with the .300. Upon raising the rifle and looking through the scope, he saw a mess of what looked like black spaghetti. When he called the custom installer about it, Miller was informed that he'd let the sun shine directly through the scope, melting the plastic cross hairs. (The "wires" were plastic because soldering melted the connections of the original Leupold reticle.)

The duplex-style reticle (introduced by Leupold under that name) is preferable for almost all hunting.

The reason, of course, is that the reticle lies at one of the two exact focal points inside the scope. When the scope points at the sun (which can happen when the rifle leans against a tree or rests across your back as you sit down), the sunlight focuses on the reticle, which melts exactly like a leaf burning under a magnifying glass.

During the early years of the plastic revolution, some scope makers tried all-plastic reticles. Cross hairs simply disappeared when melted, but one scope used a plastic post that often began to lean like the Tower of Pisa. Other shooters have experienced the sudden evaporation of add-on dots made of epoxy. Even metal cross hairs, too, can melt, particularly those made of thin foil.

Most of today's reticles are made of wire or are etched on flat glass. As mentioned in the chapter on variables, the glass reticle was pioneered by Bausch & Lomb in its early Balvars to solve the problem of the "growing" first-plane reticle. There's one small disadvantage to this method, and that is etching fine lines is how we cut glass. If the scope takes a hard hit, the reticle can break into four quarter-circles. I've heard of this happening, but usually with steel-tubed scopes, enough stiffer than aluminum to transmit shock directly to the reticle.

Leupold's Duplex is made out of platinum wire, partially flattened to produce the thick portion of the reticle. Platinum costs more than steel wire, but has both the strength and flexibility to withstand hard whacks and magnum recoil. Other common reticle materials include glass fiber, tungsten, and some softer wires like aluminum and brass. At least one maker uses a thick aluminum foil.

It's odd, but as we rapidly approach the perfection of the laser rangefinder, all of a sudden more rangefinding reticles appear on the market. These have been around for decades, of course, and the reason is they work.

Most older rangefinding reticles used extra cross hairs like David Miller's, or extra dots, but these days the Duplex-type reticle works pretty well. The same principle is used in a (pre-laser) surveyor's transit, which is to compare a reticle with a target of known size. All you need to know is how much target the reticle covers (or, technically, subtends) at one hundred yards and the dimensions of your target. On big-game animals chest-depth is most commonly used, though on varmints like ground squirrels and prairie dogs, height (or, if they're lying down, length) works better.

Aside from bears, most North American big game comes in fairly predictable sizes, especially the animals we're likely to shoot at long range such as deer, pronghorn, wild sheep, caribou, and elk. It's long been claimed that a mature buck deer measures 18 inches through the chest. I've hunted deer from Alabama to Alaska, in areas where a big mature buck weighs 150 pounds on the hoof to the northern Rockies and Canadian plains where a 250-pounder is average. It doesn't seem to matter. A 140-pound whitetail from the Deep South measured 17 inches, while my heaviest deer ever, a Montana mulie that field-dressed nearly 300 pounds, went 19 inches. The heaviest deer seem to gain much of their weight from length, not girth.

Most antelope from Montana and Wyoming (where 90 percent of the pronghorns live) measure about 15–16 inches, whether mature doe or buck. Wild sheep, bighorn or thinhorn, will measure about the same as deer. Bull caribou are about 22–24 inches through the chest, while bull elk, no matter where they're from, go about 32–35 inches.

Some mature animals vary slightly from these numbers. So what? For any long-range hunting we should be using a fast, flat-shooting cartridge. A 10 percent difference in size affects our range estimate by only 30 yards at ranges around 300. In field use the percentage is cut in half, to the 5 percent on either side of "average." This amounts to 15 yards of error at 300 yards. That won't make any significant difference whether we're shooting a 7mm-08 or a 7mm STW.

Even 10 percent error is much less than most "guesstimating," especially past 300 yards. When I guided pronghorn hunters on a regular basis, I could almost always guess ranges out to 400 yards within 25 yards or so. But that was after years of practice, in relatively flat country, on bright animals in open daylight. Often we're guessing in dim light or snow, against rocks or timber.

Even experienced hunters can't guess distances well enough to be useful. Once I took part in a range-judging contest with other writers who had hunted all over the world. Some misjudged ranges as much as 40 percent, and the average was 15 percent. These guesses were made on a sunny day while looking at posts along a road, not deer standing across a canyon in the dim light of dawn. Using a

This is a Zeiss erector tube, showing a typical European reticle featuring three heavy posts.

scope on game like antelope, deer, and elk rarely results in an error of more than 5 percent.

It's too bad more people don't use the reticles already in their scopes. The last time I used my reticle was up in Alaska, while hunting the Mulchatna caribou herd. Ray Oeltgen of Leupold and I were hunting with a guide who shall remain anonymous since he was otherwise highly competent. About noon on a misty day we found a nice bull, just out of velvet, bedded with several other bulls across a small canyon. There was just enough willow brush for a stalk around the head of the canyon, but we ran out of cover several hundred yards from the herd.

Ray was shooting his trusted old Remington 700 in .30-06, using Federal factory loads with 180-grain Nosler Partitions, sighted-in at 200 yards. As we bellied up behind the last low willows, the big bull stood up to feed, his fresh-peeled antlers washed pink by the light rain. Ray and I had talked about using reticles as rangefinders just a couple of days before, and he asked: "How far is he, John?"

I had a plain old 4X on my old .338. Knowing the average mature caribou is about 24 inches through the chest, I compared the broadside bull to the "space" between the intersection of the cross hairs and the thick bottom post of the Duplex. In the Leupold 4X, this is 7½ inches at 100 yards. The bull's chest from back to brisket "fit" that space, with just a little daylight to spare. The cross hairs-to-post distance would subtend 22½ inches at 300 yards.

I thought for a second, looking through the scope. "I'd say 350 yards."

"Bull----," the guide said. "That bull's no more than 200 yards away."

I looked through my scope again, just to make sure, then shrugged. "The cross hairs don't lie."

He and Ray thought they could crawl a little closer, so they wiggled about 25 yards ahead across the tundra. I decided to stay behind. I could see the guide talking earnestly to Ray, but couldn't hear what he was saying. Then Ray took a steady prone position and shot.

I heard the crack of bullet against bone, and the bull started hobbling around on a broken front leg. Ray shot again and missed. His third shot dropped the bull.

It turned out that once the guide had Ray away from me and my crazy theories about scopes and rangefinding, he talked him into the 200-yard range estimate. So Ray aimed right on the bull's shoulder, and the bullet broke the front leg just below the body. He even held that way for the second shot. On the third he held on the bull's backline, and the Nosler went through the bull's lungs. We paced off the distance at about 325 yards.

So much for listening to your guide in strange country. Actually, I've found most guides don't have any more clue than a Labrador retriever about judging distances, especially in mountains and odd weather. If you feel you can't afford a laser rangefinder, use your scope. That guide now does.

These days you can buy several scopes with fancy circles and "mil dots" and other graduated reticles for help in rangefinding and windage in long-range shooting. The Lightforce and Sheperd, in particular, get a lot of press. But both scopes are big and heavy, their reticles are extremely complex, and, to be honest, I have not heard great things about their ruggedness.

For big game out to the long ranges of, say, 300 to maybe 400 yards, I find such complicated reticles too cluttered; the standard Leupold Duplex and its variations seem to work just fine. Some scopes have featured a Duplex with some sort of range indicator built in. Redfield's Accutrac had a graduated post that showed the range after you bracketed the game in the reticle, while Leupold's Vari-X IIIs have additional numbers on the magnification ring that indicate yardage. The Vari-X IIIs are based on a 100-yard subtension of 16 inches, which works perfectly with pronghorns but will have to be adjusted with other animals.

But the complex reticles do fine work for varmint shooting, where you often must hold not just for range but also for wind. A good mil-dot scope, for instance, can turn an accurate .22 rimfire into a 200-yard ground-squirrel rifle. Even a standard Duplex works, the top of the bottom post often supplying an aiming point. One practical note: When using mil-dots or the bottom post of a Duplex as your aiming point, turning the magnification down can precisely resight the scope at longer ranges because with less magnification there's more subtension between the cross hairs and the post. As long as you can still see the target, this trick works wonders.

Another oft-heard objection to reticle range estimation is that game doesn't stand around to be measured. Well, if a deer's far enough away to need an accurate range estimation, it usually isn't aware of the hunter. If it is, you've done something wrong.

Some hunters say they have too many rifles and can't keep track of all the reticle measurements in their scopes. My good friend Bill McRae devised a simple solution for this, which, like a common thief, I ripped off for my own use. Bill places one of those adhesive-backed paper dots on each of his scopes, writes down the reticle measurement, then uses Scotch tape to keep the weather off. This provides an instant field reference.

Generally, I measure the reticle at 6X (or the top magnification if the scope doesn't go that high) and leave my scopes on that power for range finding. If you're really worried about the reticle measurement changing in a variable, a first-focal-plane reticle is the answer since the reticle's size doesn't change in relationship to the target.

Many scope makers now publish reticle subtension in their catalogs, but individual scopes can vary and models change. My backyard has a 2-foot piece of 1x4 nailed to the back fence, exactly 33 yards from an upstairs window, marked with lines one inch apart. I look through the scope, see how many inches a reticle subtends, then multiply by three. If that sounds too weird (or your neighbors object), most sight-in targets come marked in 1-inch squares these days. Simply measure your reticle subtension while sighting-in. Recently, scopes designed specifically for turkey hunting have become all the rage; most use a circle that encompasses a big gobbler's body at 40 yards.

All of this is good. Today's scopes help us place our shots more precisely for cleaner kills and more humane hunting. Why use the same system Neanderthals did when estimating range? A much more precise solution is right there in most scopes, if we'll only use it.

SCOPE
MOUNTS

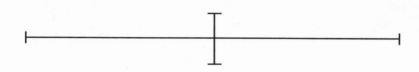

When I first developed a reputation as a gun loony shortly after I turned ten, a friend of my father's gave me several *Shooter's Bibles* and an old hardcover book on rifles. The name of that volume has long since disappeared into the same vortex that swallowed all those Top 40 song lyrics I memorized in 1966, but I do remember the chapter about telescopic sights, which made combining a scope with a rifle seem as technical as drilling for oil. It not only detailed how to shim, file, and otherwise deform scope mounts in order to get the cross hairs somewhere near the center of view, but it also described how to tap adjustment housings back and forth to adjust parallax.

Thankfully, non-centered cross hairs have gone the way of "Yummy Yummy Yummy I've Got Love In My Tummy." Many of today's shooters have never seen a scope with cross hairs centered in the northwest quadrant of the field of view. But my correspondence shows that some shooters still have troubles getting scopes satisfactorily mounted on their rifles.

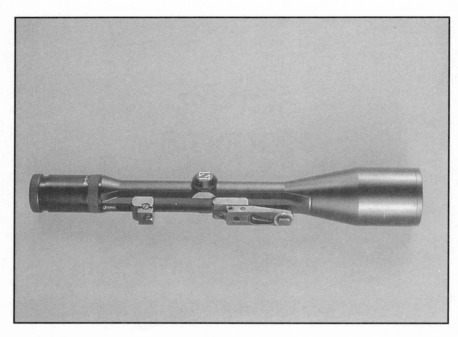

This Zeiss rail mount is detachable and very repeatable, but costs about $600 total for the mount and installation.

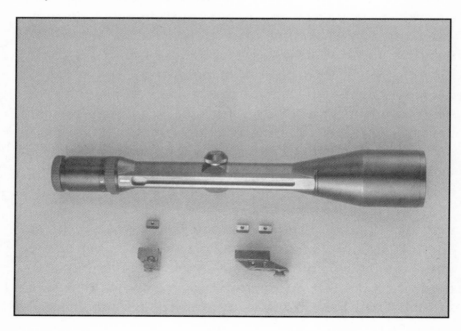

S<small>COPE</small> M<small>OUNTS</small>

Many of these difficulties can be avoided, especially if you mount your own scope. Once upon a time in the dark ages, when we existed without e-mail and sun-dried tomatoes, rifles weren't drilled and tapped for scope-mounting screws, and had bolt handles, safeties, and ejection ports that interfered with a top-mounted scope.

Today most center-fire and rimfire rifles (and even many handguns and muzzleloaders) come ready to accept scopes. Nowadays the problem isn't the firearm; modern scopes come in as many sizes and shapes as Sport Utility Vehicles. We have compact scopes, varmint scopes, huge-objective scopes, and scopes with 1-inch and 30mm tubes.

I do a lot of fooling with rifles and constantly switch scopes, either to test rifles or to find The Perfect Scope to match The Perfect Rifle. In these tangled journeys with screwdriver and Loc-Tite, I've found many strange things. Twenty or thirty years ago, about any scope would mate with any rifle. But today far fewer scopes will mount satisfactorily, which means as low as possible, with proper eye relief, with all mounts on all rifles.

Sometimes the adjustment turrets are in the wrong place, the magnification ring interferes with the bolt handle, or the mounts aren't high enough to keep the objective lens off the barrel. As Roseanne Rosannadanna used to say, "It's always *something*." For a while Bausch & Lomb even made several scopes too short to fit in the standard mounts of the long-action Ruger 77, one of America's most popular bolt rifles. Burris still makes a few scopes with so little tube between the adjustment turrets and the objective bell that you simply cannot use Weaver rings, perhaps the most popular scope mount of all time. Are the engineers who design these things selected from a list of people who have never seen a rifle? Or are they imported from some Russian farm where they've been devising new potato famines?

I've also tried most of the mounts on the market today and have yet to find one that doesn't work for at least some scopes (though I *have* encountered a few that are almost impossible to put together, unless you have three hands). So how do you choose a scope mount? There are several considerations, including cost, height, weight, looks, strength, ring spacing, and whether the scope can be removed and replaced while retaining zero.

Many hunters automatically choose the one-piece base, sometimes called the bridge mount because it bridges the ejection port of a bolt-action rifle. (Here I must point out that the original term meant any mount that allowed the scope to bridge the top of the action—in essence, any low and central top mount, even with two-piece bases.) These look tougher than woodpecker lips, which is why many folks like them.

Looks can deceive, however. Almost all one-piece bases mount with only three screws, versus four in the two-piece bases. No chain is stronger than its weakest link, and the minuscule (search for one in a shag rug sometime) 6-48 base screws are the weak link in scope mounts.

One-piece bases have other drawbacks. The all-time standard, the Redfield JR, can weigh 8 ounces with its rings, and even the lighter Conetrol mount weighs close to 6 ounces. In contrast, a set of Weaver rings and bases goes about 3 1/2 ounces. If the rifle's screw holes aren't drilled exactly (yes, this happens, even in computer-operated America), the base can bend the receiver slightly, creating all sorts of strange and frustrating accuracy problems. Bridge mounts also prevent you from carrying the rifle by the scope. This may seem an odd thing to do, but with a good scope and mount it doesn't hurt a thing, and turns out to be very comfortable and practical in open country.

On the plus side, one-piece bases often allow the rear scope ring to be mounted farther forward than two-piece bases. This gives more leeway in mounting scopes, especially compacts. The question in the back of my mind, however, is why would anyone pair a 9-ounce scope with a mount that weighs darn near the same?

By now you may suspect that I don't like one-piece bases. Unless they're required for some special need, you're absolutely correct. Others I have little use for are the European claw-and-rail mounts. These are designed for quick and reliable scope removal and replacement. In general they work very well but are heavy, really expensive, and won't do any job that much cheaper, simpler American-style mounts perform perfectly.

But Europeans have a different view of such things, perhaps because only a very tiny percentage of Europeans hunt. In Germany hunters make up less than a half-percent of the total population, while in the US about 7 percent of

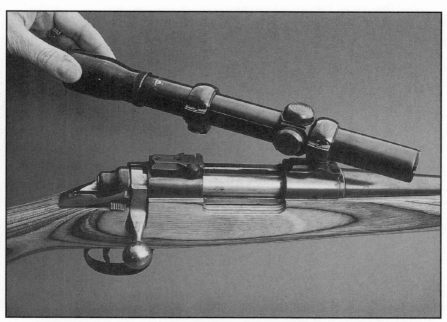

The Redfield-type mount is probably the most popular. This is a Burris Signature, with plastic ring inserts that help align the scope.

us hunt. What this boils down to is that only rich Germans hunt. This tends to skew the thinking on sporting arms.

While I was on a tour of the Zeiss factories in 1993 with other gunwriters, we also visited a gunshop where the owner installed one of Zeiss's new rail mounts. We watched for a half-hour or so while the gunsmith seemingly made a small amount of rather insubstantial progress. Meanwhile one of the Zeiss officials told of the advantages of this mount—mostly, as I recall, that it was absolutely perfect. Among other things, you had to buy a special railed Zeiss scope, as well as the mount, then pay a German gunsmith to attach the thing. Would American shooters be interested in such a marvelous mount?

"How much does it cost?" one of us asked. Maybe it was me.

"Oh, about 900 Deutsche marks. Six-hundred dollars."

"NO!" sang a chorus of gunwriters.

The classic European claw mount has been around a long time. This Mannlicher rifle features an old Zeiss scope with a huge objective lens.

So if you really want claw or rail mounts, you're on your own. Instead, let's look at two-piece mounts.

These can be broken down into six categories: steel, Weaver, all-aluminum, detachable, see-through, and integral. Each has its strong and weak points.

The two most common all-steel mounts are the Redfield SR (including several interchangeable with it, like the Leupold, Burris, and Millett) and Conetrol. There are also at least two variations on the Conetrol theme, Dave Gentry's and S&K's. There are also a few designs that resemble nothing but themselves, like the Buehler and Tasco World Class.

Blued all-steel mounts are considered good-looking, especially the Conetrol and its derivatives and are, therefore, often chosen for custom or classic rifles. The heaviest are the Redfield and Buehler (now made by another company under the Buehler name) at 5½ ounces including bases and rings. The Conetrol and Millett come in at just over 4 ounces, with the S&K around 3½ ounces and Dave Gentry's latest Feather-Lights under 3.

Most of these mounts feature windage adjustment, which was critical in the days when scope-mounting holes were often crooked, usually thanks to a shade-tree gunsmith. These days windage adjustment can still come in handy when mounting scopes with a narrow adjustment range, particularly high-power varmint scopes—or when a factory rifle arrives with a barrel slightly cockeyed in the action. This does happen, more than once a leap year.

All of these mounts are fairly complex and pretty darn strong. Some allow detaching and replacing the scope with accuracy. The problem with using a Redfield-type mount as a detachable lies in the front dovetail, which loosens after a number of removals. The only real cure is another base and ring. If you intend to take the scope on and off more than once every year or two, a detachable mount designed for the job is probably a better idea.

The Leupold detachable mount is very rugged, since it features studs that fit into holes in the bases. The scope is a Burris with an extremely short front-tube section. This can cause real problems with Weaver mounts but not with most clamshell-type rings, where a top half is screwed onto the bottom half.

Many of these mounts allow some latitude in the scopes they'll accept. Most offer several ring heights, though without the exact scope and several pairs of rings it's often hard to imagine how combinations can fail. For instance, the power-change ring on variables often requires a higher ring when everything else fits. Some makers offer a reversible front base, allowing for shorter or longer scopes. The lightest Redfield-type is the Millett; it gets light with shortened bases, allowing less variation in scopes.

For big-game rifles my favorite nondetachable, all-steel mount is the Conetrol and its variations, which are light, strong, and good looking. The bases usually allow a wide latitude in scope lengths. The Conetrol's rings are made in three parts—two halves and a cap that holds them together—while the Gentry and S&K mounts feature one-piece rings. These actually bend around the scope tube, forming an unbroken ring. The rings of all three mounts clamp around the scope tube, at the bottom forming a stud that fits into a hole in the base, providing perhaps the best combination of strength versus weight on the market.

Weaver mounts also clamp around the scope and are also very light, partly because the bases and bottom halves of the rings are aluminum. Some hunters put down aluminum in scope mounts, but Weavers hold up very well even on hard-kicking rifles. I've used Weaver mounts on an 8½-pound (with scope) .416 Remington without any problems. The original action holes and bases were redrilled and tapped for 8-40 screws (a good idea on all heavy-kicking rifles). The rings were also fitted with longer 8-40 screws. This is more easily done with the Weaver than with steel models, and the larger screws are easier to find.

Weaver rings were originally designed to be detachable and withstand removal and replacement as accurately as any mounts designed around each ring clamping to a base. The trick in accurately remounting Weavers is to press the scope forward in the mounts, eliminating the slack that would ordinarily be taken up during recoil, then tighten the rings gradually and alternately—front and rear—until they firm up. Using this technique, Weavers replace just as precisely as any two-screw detachable mount I've ever seen.

The only problems with Weavers are down-deep ugliness and occasional mounting problems with short scopes. Weaver does make extension rings, but these are higher than their lowest standard model, which gets the scope lower than with any other brand. Other companies make rings to fit Weaver bases, some much more esthetic than Old Ugly. None works significantly better, but all are much prettier, albeit also heavier.

I've tried every two-screw detachable mount I could lay my hands on, from cheap Weavers to expensive semi-custom mounts. They all shift, unless you tighten the rings up gradually and alternately as described above. (Actually, the Redfield-type system is more accurately repeatable than most two-screw detachable designs, simply because only one screw needs to be tightened when the scope is replaced. After sighting-in, just Loc-Tite one rear base screw into place, then turn the other out when you want to remove the scope.)

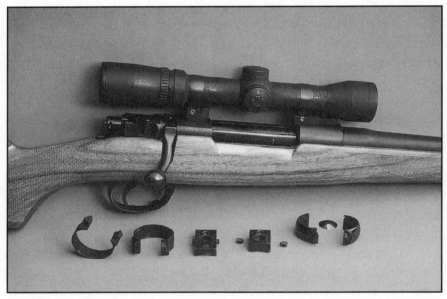

Perhaps the strongest all-steel scope mount is the Conetrol and its variations. Essentially these provide a ring of steel that clamps around the scope. The Conetrol ring (right) is made of two halves and has a cap that holds them together; the Gentry ring (left) is a flexible piece of steel that wraps around the scope. Both form a stud at the bottom of the ring that fits into a hole in the base (center). The stud is held by opposing screws (shown lying next to right base) that allow windage adjustment of both front and rear mounts. Not only is this system strong and reasonably adjustable, but it also looks good and weighs less than most Redfield-type mounts. The original Conetrol weighs about four ounces, while Dave Gentry's variation weighs less than three.

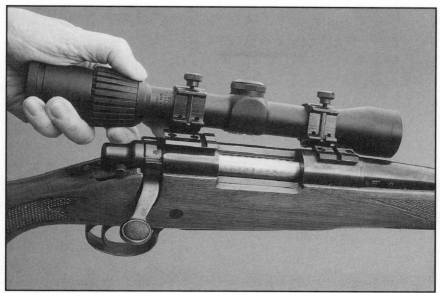

The cheapest popular mount on the market is the Weaver. Aside from economy, its virtues are light weight (about 3½ ounces in most models) and detachability. In fact, it replaces just as accurately as other detachable mounts that cost three to ten times as much. There's no better choice when using a hunting rifle in distant and rugged places, because a backup scope can be affordably set up in another set of rings.

Among other clamp-style detachables, Talley rings are probably the most popular among lovers of fine rifles. The instructions that accompany the mounts are also the only ones I've seen suggesting the alternate tightening of the two ring clamps when remounting the scope.

They are also very precisely made mounts. After centering the reticle on the scope I used to test the mounts, I mounted the scope in the rings, set the scope on the bases, tightened everything down, stuck a collimator in the muzzle, and found the cross hairs about 2 inches from the center of the collimator grid. This is highly unusual. Talleys also have the stoutest recoil shoulder among the clamp-style detachables.

The European rail mount is ideal for takedown rifles.

There is one other thing to think about if you desire clamp-type detachables. Those nifty-looking levers that many detachables feature get caught on everything, both in the woods and on your clothing. If the scope's mounted right, you won't be able to move them by finger pressure anyway. That's why most experienced hunters prefer coin-slotted screw heads rather than levers—if they prefer detachables at all.

The integral mount, with rings that clamp directly to grooves or dovetails in the rifle action, is a really good idea that also usually provides a decent detachable system. Unfortunately, the only commercial rifles I know of that feature it today are the Sako and Ruger. Aftermarket rings—some including windage adjustments—are also available for the Ruger. The only problem lies in that some scopes will not fit the ring spacing. You can buy extension rings, but, as with the Weaver, these usually raise the height of the scope.

The Warne differs from other two-screw detachables by offering a rear base with an integral peep sight. This is one of the handiest combinations for really rugged or wet country, and the bases are low enough to see the darn iron sights, too. I have one of these on my .375, and it works very slickly.

Instead of two screws that tighten rings to bases, the Leupold detachable features heavy studs on the bottom of each ring. These slide into holes in the bases, and tighten with what amount to wedges. They're more repeatable than any clamp-type detachable, and after they've been taken on and off a few times they repeat even more reliably. Because of the stud and locking mechanism, however, the bases are, like those of many detachables, very high.

High bases are my rabid complaint about too many elegant and otherwise practical detachable mounts. The only really valid reason for any detachable is that it permits the relatively quick use of iron sights, whether open or peep. But just try to see most iron sights over the high bases of almost every model except the Weaver. The trough along the middle of each Weaver base allows a better look at open sights than any other detachable on the market.

I guess what it all comes down to is that most people who buy detachable mounts don't use the iron sights much, if ever, especially the folks who order tricked-out custom rifles. Detachable mounts make sense only in country so wet that scopes are useless much of the time or for dangerous game in very thick brush. Unless you regularly encounter either, mount one of today's very reliable scopes low and permanently over the action, and then quit fiddling.

(This is especially true of handguns. Up to about .44 Magnum, there isn't much problem with conventional rifle-type scope mounts, even on specialty handguns like the Thompson/Center Contender in which the longer barrel often raises the velocity—and hence recoil—of even conventional handgun cartridges. Go much above .44 Magnum, however, and things start to come apart in a hurry, and these days there are dozens of much more powerful handgun rounds. Today's really hard kicking "hand rifles" often require extra rings to hold the scope in place and bases that attach with more than three or four 6-48 screws.)

A few companies make mounts in which the bottom half of the ring screws directly onto the rifle. Obviously, these work on only one rifle model, but they eliminate the screws that connect base and ring (another weak link) and most are very light. The absolute lightest is the model Melvin Forbes designed for his Ultra Light Arms rifles, coming in right at 2 ounces *with* screws. Combined with an 8-ounce Leupold 1–4X, these create a scope/mount combo of about 10 ounces, less than most 4X scopes. The J. B. Holden Company makes them and also sells a general version called the Plainsman mount available for popular bolt-actions.

Holden also makes the Ironsighter—the most popular see-through mount—which allows instant use of either scope or iron sights. It's very popular in country where rain or wet snow can make it tough to use a scope. It does, necessarily, mount the scope very high, and the height also weakens the mount somewhat, but the Ironsighter works as advertised.

Beyond the basic categories of Redfield, Conetrol, and Weaver, the variations in rifle mounts are almost endless. I once did a call-in radio show on optics, and almost half the questions were versions of: "I have a 1937 Albanian military rifle and want to mount a scope on it. Where can I get mounts?" Damned if I know, though I'd bet the Brownells gunsmithing catalog would list it. If you are going to do any amount of your own gunsmithing, which includes scope mounting, you need a Brownells catalog. You will find just about every scope mount available listed. If you have a question, call them not me.

SCOPE
MOUNTING

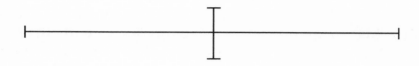

After you decide on a mount, the next trick is combining scope and rifle. I've read articles that make this process seem as complicated as computer programming, even with the most straightforward mount designs. Done right, scope mounting is more involved than changing your car's oil, but not by much.

Of course, you can pay a gunsmith to do the job, and most sporting-goods stores mount scopes free when you buy them. Neither solution sets up the scope for your style of shooting. I have seen supposedly "professional" jobs shake loose within a week of hard hunting, along with cross hairs 10 or 15 degrees off-kilter. If whoever does the mounting doesn't know what he's about (a real possibility, especially in sporting-goods stores just before hunting season), common Redfield-type mounts can stress the scope more than an IRS audit. This is a real and unseen factor in many shooting problems. So, if you are at all mechanically inclined, it's a good idea to mount your own scopes. It will take far longer for me to describe doing it right than for you to perform the job.

For many popular commercial rifles and mounts, particularly the Conetrol and most variations on the Redfield, all you'll need are some cotton swabs and Loc-Tite (buy the type that allows you to take the mount apart later if you want to). Most of these mounts come with hex or Torx screws these days and include a wrench.

Weaver mounts and some others require the correct screwdriver. The "correct" screwdriver means that the flats of the blades are parallel and the tip precisely fits the slot, in both depth and width. Scope-mount screws tend to be relatively soft—soft screws hold better—and anything less than a nearly perfect screwdriver will rip the heads up rather than tighten them. If you intend to do more than a little gun tinkering, a good interchangeable-tip gunsmithing screwdriver like those sold by Brownells is a cheap investment. For Weavers and most other slot-screw mounts, you can also use a cheap hardware-store screwdriver with a $3/16$-inch shaft. Cut the regular tip off with a hacksaw, then file or grind a new tip to fit the screws.

Put your unloaded rifle in a vise padded with leather or inner-tube rubber. If it's a new rifle, remove the filler screws. This requires a tiny screwdriver, like the one that comes as part of a kit for eyeglasses. You can even file the tip of a metal nail file to fit, since these screws aren't usually very tight.

Clean and degrease the holes. If you pull most of the cotton off a Q-Tip and run the swab into the holes, you'll get 90 percent of the oil out. Then degrease with a little soapy water or rubbing alcohol. This helps the screws and Loc-Tite hold better.

Next, lay the bases from your mount on the rifle. Hold the scope above the bases and see if the rings will allow adequate spacing. Some bases are reversible and allow more

Here a pair of Brownells aligning rods are being used to line up a pair of Redfield-style rings on a Browning single-shot .243.

latitude. You want the rings to support the scope as near the objective and eyepiece bells as possible. This helps prevent the scope from bending if you and the rifle fall down, or if it gets beaten up by a horse.

Degrease the screws, then place them in the mounts. Many mounts require longer screws for the rear base than for the front; try not to mix them up. Then screw the bases on—not supertight—just firmly enough to make sure the screws fit and the holes in the bases aren't clogged and actually have threads. Threadless holes do occur, and more frequently these days.

Now try to operate the rifle's action. Occasionally, base screws intrude into the action enough to bind the bolt, locking lugs, or other works. This means you have to grind or file a thread or two off the offending screw. Again, this doesn't occur very often with popular rifles or mounts. But to paraphrase an ex-president, doo-doo happens.

If everything's copacetic, back the screws out and prepare to cinch things down. If you hunt much in wet weather, you might pick this moment to apply some car wax to the bottom of the base and the top of the rifle's action to prevent rust. Surface tension will suck water right into the thin joint between base and rifle and cause rust under there where you can't see it, even if your action is made of "stainless" steel.

If everything's OK, slip the screws into one of the bases and apply a tiny bit of Loc-Tite to the threads poking out the bottom of the base. It's better to do this than to drip Loc-Tite in the action holes; a "blind" hole filled with liquid may prevent the screw from bottoming. Then screw the base down, as tightly as you can, without mangling the screw holes. Do the same with the other base.

Now mount the bottom halves of the rings on the bases. (The only exceptions to this step involve dovetail mounts like Ruger's or the Conetrol and its variations.) With Redfield-type rings, the front ring fits into a dovetail slot that must be turned 90 degrees to lock. So here you must put together the ring to gain some leverage.

In new mounts, it's best to turn the ring with a plastic or wooden lever that will fit inside the ring. I normally use a small screwdriver handle, but a foot-long, 1-inch hardwood dowel is ideal.

Do not use your scope to turn the ring on new mounts. Some folks (including most mount and scope manufacturers) say *never* use the scope to turn the ring, but that's how all the detachable modifications of the Redfield system work. After the dovetail is broken in, there's no real harm in using the scope to turn the ring.

Turn the ring until it lines up perpendicular to the bore. This is where many scope mounters screw up. If the front ring is off square, you'll either dent the scope or create strange stresses when everything's tightened up.

The best solution is to also mount the rear ring, in the opposing screws on the rear base, then use a 1-inch dowel or pipe as a substitute scope tube to line things up. Or use the aligning rods that Brownells sells. These are a pair of solid aluminum cylinders with sharp cones at one end. You mount them in the rings with the cones pointing toward each other (see photo) and tweak the rings until the points of the cones line up precisely. Really professional scope mounters have these in their tool kit. They only cost about twenty bucks, so if you mount more than one scope a year they're another good investment.

Once you get the front and rear rings lined up, remove the tops of the rings and place the scope in the bottom halves. Then screw down the ring tops until there's just enough tension to hold the scope in place. You should be able to slide it back and forth, however, since this is where we adjust for eye relief.

Sometimes there isn't much choice because either the scope tube will just fit between the rings, or there won't be much tube between the adjustment turrets and the lens bells. If there's any room at all, sit down and aim the rifle before tightening the rings down. Slide the scope back and forth until the view is optimum.

Sitting is a compromise. From offhand your eye will be slightly farther from the scope, but from prone it will be a little closer. This is one reason I like long, noncritical eye relief. Short eye relief means your eye must be in absolutely the same position behind the scope to get a full field of view.

Also, twist the scope until the cross hairs are level, making sure there's an adjustment turret on the right side of the scope as you aim the rifle. One friend, an experienced shotgunner new to rifles, mounted a 4X Leupold on his new .270. He shot up three boxes of factory ammo before somebody pointed out that he was trying to adjust elevation with the windage knob, and vice versa.

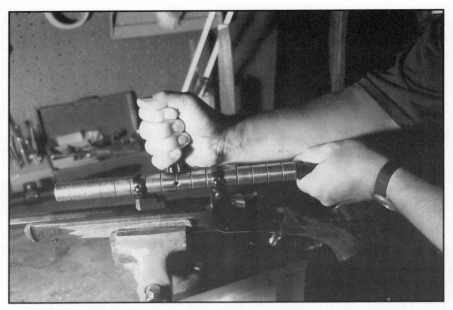

For the most perfectly aligned, stress-free scope mounting, the rings should be lapped. Here the job is being done with a Brownells' lapping rod.

(There are rare variations in the placement of the windage turret. Simmons's very fine V-Tac varmint scope, for instance, has the windage knob on the left side of the scope, where right-handed shooters can adjust it while aiming the rifle.)

Some people have a terrible time getting the cross hairs level, and some experienced hunters actually prefer them a little canted, since they naturally cant the rifle. I hold the rifle at arm's length and try to center the vertical cross hair with the center of a rifle's bolt, or the center of the rear mount on actions other than bolts. There's at least one device on the market that helps cross hair alignment, if you really need help.

Now, tighten down the ring screws. Some people use Loc-Tite on these, too, but the natural springiness of a scope's aluminum tube keeps some tension on ring screws. I've never had them work loose, as frequently happens with bare base screws. And it is possible to clamp rings down too tightly, freezing a variable's inner works.

Tighten down the screws alternately, as you would the lug nuts on a car—first the left rear, then the right front, then the right rear, etc. Tighten them only a little at a time, trying to keep the gap between the top and bottom of the ring even. There's always a little stress on the scope after a mounting job—one of the reasons it takes a few shots for some rifles to "settle down." This rotating, gradual tightening of the screws minimizes that stress and also helps keep the scope square with the rifle. If you just tighten the rear right-hand screw down all the way, your carefully aligned cross hairs will be out of line. Check the reticle alignment again after everything's tight.

Now you're ready for bore-sighting. For the absolute best results, center the cross hairs in the scope beforehand. This is done by turning each adjustment dial until it stops, then turning it the other way, counting the turns, until it stops again. Then turn the dial half that number of turns.

Centering the reticle before adjusting the mount does two things. First, it provides the maximum amount of scope adjustment for sighting-in. Second, the optical center of the lens system provides the brightest and clearest view. And if the scope's really out of alignment, you can also have parallax problems.

Center both the vertical and horizontal adjustments, then bore-sight the scope, either with a collimator or by actually looking through the bore at some small object at least twenty-five yards away. If you don't have a collimator or a vise anywhere near a window, use a cardboard box with notches cut for the fore-end and butt. All you need is some rig to hold the rifle steady while you can compare the view through the bore and the scope.

Obviously, this system won't work with lever, pump, and semiauto rifles in which you can't look through the bore. The best solution here is to borrow a collimator, or actually shoot the rifle at twenty-five or thirty yards, doing the initial adjusting with the mount's windage screws rather than the scope itself. With Redfield-type mounts, it's easy to adjust for windage by turning the rear screws in and out. With most of today's factory rifles and mounts, the horizontal elevation should be very close. If it's not, you'll have to shim one of the bases or use Burris's Signature rings.

Shims are easy to make out of aluminum beverage cans. These can be cut with scissors (not good sewing scissors). If the scope points very low, then you have to shim the front base; if very high, shim the rear base. I must emphasize *very* here. What we are doing is only approximately lining up the scope and barrel, using the scope's adjustments for fine-tuning.

When using Redfield-style bases, I have about given up using anything but Signature rings. These feature a ball-and-socket type "joint" in each ring, filled with a plastic ring that comes in two halves. Each mount comes with several of these plastic rings, identified by numbers like +5, -10, or 0. These indicate how much each plastic ring offsets the scope tube. In effect, you're shimming the inside of each scope ring instead of the bases. They work, and very slickly. In addition to allowing adjustment in the mount, they won't mar your scope. Signature rings are a simple and marvelous solution to a longtime problem.

With Conetrol-type mounts, there's windage adjustment in both front and rear rings. The only real problem with putting Conetrols together is just that—putting them together. Conetrol rings come in three pieces, two sides and a cap that locks the two sides together. And once you get the rings on the scope, it's sometimes almost impossible to level the cross hairs or move the scope back and forth. This is especially difficult with matte rings and a matte scope, though not usually a problem with glossy rings and scopes.

The Gentry and S&K variations use a one-piece ring that you simply wrap around the scope. This works as slick as river rocks. Both models are slightly more expensive, however, and not quite as good-looking as Conetrols, at least to my eye.

With any of the three, the bottom of the ring forms a split stud that fits into a hole in the base. Two opposing screws in the base tighten the ring and provide the windage adjustments.

With Weaver rings, and some others, there is no windage adjustment. You can shim them, of course, for vertical correction. But the only real solution for noticeable horizontal misalignment is custom bases with the holes drilled off-center. Weaver makes blank bases for just this reason, and if you've got a drill press you can probably do the job yourself. If not, you have to visit a gunsmith.

If the vertical cross hair still won't line up, something is very wrong. On sporterized military rifles the mounting holes were probably drilled crooked. You can get holes welded up and redrilled, but this often involves reheat-treatment and other expensive procedures. Often it's easier to get the action redrilled for a side mount.

New rifles usually have their barrels screwed in crooked. Send these back to the manufacturer, or take them back to the store.

Once in a while the mount, not the rifle, may be the problem. Sometimes defective bases leave the factory, but more probably it's the wrong model. Mixups occasionally happen in ordering and packaging. Most often they occur when the dingbat behind the counter at the local discount store cannot read or doesn't care.

The only real trick with Weaver rings is getting the scope's cross hairs level. The tightening screws are all on one side of the rings, so when you cinch things down the cross hairs tilt slightly. Some people evidently think this is normal, but it's easy to fix. Just note how far out of square the cross hairs tilt, then back off the ring screws slightly. Twist the scope about that far the other way and tighten the screws down again. It may take two or three tries to get things square, but it can be done.

Other rings on the market, like the Talley and the Warne, all come with instructions that are pretty straightforward. If all else fails, read the instructions first. I am only an average mechanic, but I have been completely baffled by only one mount that evidently needed two people to hold things together while a third tightened the screws.

If you're truly an accuracy nut, then you'll probably want to lap the rings. This takes out the last little bit of misalignment inherent in any ring system except Burris Signatures. The job itself is pretty easy, done by loosely mounting a 1-inch or 30mm metal rod in the scope rings as if the rod were a scope that still needed to be adjusted for eye relief. Then a medium-coarse abrasive is applied to the rod and the rod is slid back and forth in the rings. Once the rod starts to slide easily, the rings are tightened a little. The process continues until the rings fit the rod perfectly. Then the rings are cleaned and the scope is mounted totally free of any stress. If you can't find a rod of the right size, Brownells sells a Scope Ring Alignment lap with handles on the side and end that makes quick work of the job.

Sometimes, despite the grand schemes of mount designers and your own skill, scopes will slide in the rings during recoil. Some rings feature tape to hold things tight; some are scored or grooved. If not, the best solution I've tried is the rubber gasket-forming cement sold in auto-supply stores. Like most of the really handy techniques in this book, this one was stolen from somebody else, in this case gunwriter-par-excellence Ross Seyfried. Knowing Ross, he has probably already found something better, but I haven't.

SCOPE ADJUSTMENT AND SIGHTING-IN

Once your scope and rifle are one, you can experience the highs and lows of scope adjustments. These days there are far more good times, thanks to better scope mechanics in general. But once in a while things still don't work out as simply as turning the knobs seven clicks up and three to the right.

Whether through simple bore-sighting or the use of a collimator, you should begin the process of matching reticle to bullet impact by exactly aligning the cross hairs with the rifle's bore. Most scope adjustments are much better than those of a generation ago, but still the clicks sometimes don't move the reticle exactly as claimed. It is good to know this before going to the range. I test new scopes on my Bushnell collimator, which features a grid with squares measuring the equivalent of 4 inches at 100 yards. If each of a scope's clicks is supposed to move the cross hairs ¼ inch, then 16 clicks should move them one square. In using any collimator, barrel length can affect the exact amount of each click, but standard bolt-action

For proper sight-in a sturdy benchrest is essential. Here Eileen Clarke shoots a Remington 700 in .338 over a bench-top nailed to posts buried two feet in the ground.

rifles with 22- to 24-inch barrels usually match up pretty well with any good collimator.

After mounting the collimator in the muzzle, I center the cross hairs, then turn the adjustments until the cross hairs have moved one square. If the scope supposedly has ¼-inch clicks (each click moves the point of impact ¼ inch at 100 yards, fairly standard these days on big game scopes), this should take 16 clicks both horizontally and vertically. Sometimes this works out just right, and sometimes it doesn't; for some reason, often the clicks move the cross hairs more like ⅓ inch.

It really doesn't matter. What does matter is repeatability. The adjustments should move the cross hairs the same amount each time. When I turn the adjustment dials back up and over the same number of clicks, the cross hairs should be right back in the center of the collimator's grid.

The handy thing about a collimator is that you can look through the scope while making adjustments to see if the darn cross hairs move with each click. If they don't, something's wrong, and you'll have about as much fun sighting-in as an Inuit would on a visit to Death Valley. You can perform the same test when bore-sighting, though it will not be quite as precise. Or, like some gunwriters, you can go to the range and burn up a box of ammo while testing click accuracy. I prefer the collimator.

The adjustments on modern scopes consist of a screw on the top and another on the right side of the erector tube. Inside the scope, pressing the erector tube against these screws, is a spring or two. Turning the screws in and out should make the tube move sideways or up and down. If you turn each screw to the right, as you would when tightening a bolt, the screw is normally pushing against the erector tube. Consequently these adjustments (down and left on almost all scopes) are usually very reliable.

Most problems occur when we need the rifle's shots to go up and right because then the springs need to push the erector tube against the retreating screw. If the springs are a little weak, the cross hairs may not move or may move suddenly or slowly after the dial is turned.

So strong springs are needed for reliable adjustments. Until recently, the Europeans seemed to understand this fact better than many American and Japanese manufacturers, which is one reason their scopes had a reputation for precise and reliable adjustments. Almost all of today's scopes feature very repeatable adjustments. If they don't, there may be something wrong and the scope should be returned to the manufacturer.

A few years ago the Burris Posi-Lock was hailed as a major advancement in reliable adjustments. The system consists of a setscrew mounted at a 45-degree angle opposite the adjustment turrets, in addition to the standard springs.

After adjusting the scope, you turn the setscrew until it firms up against the erector tube, locking the erector tube against the adjustment screws. This removes all slack from the adjustments and prevents impact shift during recoil.

It works, though there is a minor impact shift when the screw is tightened. I suspect the real reason for Posi-Lock's reputation for reliability lies in Burris's insistence on using a heavy brass erector tube.

A brass tube has one big advantage over an aluminum or plastic tube: It slides slickly. Despite Burris's advertising, for all practical purposes brass is very heavy and isn't stronger than modern plastics or aircraft-grade aluminum. This not only makes Burris scopes noticeably heavier than similar models from most other makers but also creates mechanical problems in the adjustment system.

The sheer weight of the brass tube means more leverage must be applied in the scope's adjustments. I suspect this is the reason Burris's adjustment turrets lie farther forward than those of other scopes, providing more leverage. This doesn't solve the whole problem, however.

The heavy tube can also shift even under the pressure of strong springs, especially during recoil. Remember that heavier scopes mean more inertia during recoil—and more momentum once the scope gets moving. That heavy brass tube inside the scope is like a piano in a pickup bed. Even if the piano fits the pickup bed pretty well, the piano tends to slide around slightly if you stomp on the gas or suddenly lean on the brakes.

Enter the Posi-Lock, which ties down the piano. Essentially, the Posi-Lock is a solution to a problem that doesn't exist with lighter erector tubes. It works for Burris but really isn't needed on most other scopes.

In any scope, accurate and positive adjustments are usually accompanied by some effort in use and a very positive feel (or even sound) accompanying each click. If point of

For scope adjustments to be repeatable, the springs need to be strong. This means it should take firm effort to turn the dials. With the common click-type adjustments, the clicks should be easily felt and even heard.

impact doesn't change when you adjust the scope, or moves only after two or three shots, the springs are too light. The old Bausch & Lomb Bal-series was the worst I'd ever seen for this problem in quality scopes. The adjustments were marvelously easy to twirl, but very often the scope wouldn't shift until you shot the rifle. In cold weather, any adjustment would often mean a vertical or horizontal stringing of three or four shots as the scope caught up with where you had turned it. The new B&L Elites are much better in this respect. Their adjustments are inevitably much harder to turn but feature a handy ridge on the dial, so you don't have to dig for a coin.

Most of today's better scopes feature almost foolproof adjustments, as evidenced by the proliferation of "target" turrets, those high knobs that can be twirled between shots. If a scope has target knobs, you can be pretty sure the adjustments are reliable; otherwise, it won't last long on the market.

If you're a traveling hunter, you should know where your rifle shoots at distances other than 100 yards. Here Johnny Unser tries his 7mm magnum at a 130-yard target in a caribou camp in Alaska.

With accurate, repeatable adjustments, sighting-in is a pretty straightforward process. Make sure all screws are tight on both the rifle (or handgun or slug gun) and scope mount; also make sure you're using the same ammo for each shot rather than a mixed box. Even if you've carefully bore-sighted or collimated the rifle, shooting at short range before trying the 100-yard target can save tempers and ammunition. The standard suggestion is 25 yards, but I prefer 30 to 35. This comes closer to lining up the shots an inch or two high at 100 yards than shooting at 25 yards, which often results in shots 6 to 12 inches high at 100 yards, depending on the height of the mount and the speed of the bullet.

Always rest the rifle's fore-end on something soft. Unless asked to, I never comment on other people's shooting at the range. I had to bite my tongue real hard last fall, when two old buddies were trying to sight-in their .30-30s

Proper sighting-in is critical for any big-game hunting, but it is most critical for long-range game like pronghorn. Bob Gerol took this nice buck in New Mexico with a .30-06 sighted in 3 inches high at 100 yards. The only problem with this sighting is the tendency for many calibers to shoot 4 inches high at ranges around 150-200 yards. Since Bob's buck was 250 yards away, there wasn't any problem.

by resting the muzzle of each rifle on a pile of 2x6s. Even at 25 yards (they never shot at 100), their "groups" resembled buckshot patterns. I just hope they never found an unlucky deer.

You don't need a professional tripod rest and rabbit ear sandbags to sight-in accurately, but you do need a bench or some steady substitute. On calm days a lowered pickup tailgate isn't bad, but in a wind (when you shouldn't be sighting-in anyway) the whole truck rocks.

Both the rifle's fore-end and buttstock should be supported. Ideally the position should be so steady that you can take your hands off the rifle and the cross hairs will still point at the target. Sometimes that's just not possible, but it's something to strive toward. You should be able to sit straight behind the rifle, or even stand (a good idea with hard kickers). The shooting should be relaxed, with no strain on you or the rifle.

Adjusting the point of impact at short range can be done with single shots, but at 100 yards shoot at least three-shot groups. Let the rifle cool between groups. Even if you've carefully measured the adjustments in your scope, don't assume that if you turn the dials 3 inches left and 2 inches high the next group will be right there. Shoot again to make sure. We're talking about hunting here, in which a shot 2 inches off at 100 yards means 6 inches off at 300 yards. As we gunwriters constantly point out, there are no benchrests in the woods, so your hold may be less than rock-steady. Six inches at 300 yards can mean a gut-shot rather than lung-shot deer.

(Here I must admit to having seen one benchrest in the woods. In Alaska a couple of years ago I had just returned to camp and was standing near to the benchrest/fish-cleaning table next to the river when a bull moose appeared 250 yards upstream, walking right toward me. I picked up my .338 from where it lay on the bank and sat down at the benchrest. The bull stopped right next to the target we'd used to sight-in, 130 yards upstream.

(Then the guide showed up and loudly—and somewhat desperately—whispered not to shoot the bull in the middle of the *#}&%$! river. The moose heard him and started up the bank. This put him behind a willow about fifty feet from me, so I had to hop down the bank and take a rest over an alder's roots. As soon as all four of the bull's hoofs were on dry land, I shot. He promptly stood up on his hind legs and fell backward into the river. And that's as close as I've ever come to shooting a big-game animal from a benchrest.)

Now that you're all sighted-in, don't believe the hunting tip about sticking a collimator in the muzzle and noting where the cross hairs are, then using the collimator when you get to hunting camp to find out if the rifle is still on. I have used different collimators over the years, and it is a disheartening experience to check the scope setting, remove the collimator, and then stick it back in the muzzle. Often the collimator screen shows that your rifle has shifted impact several inches in those few seconds. The only way you can make sure your rifle is still shooting spot-on is to shoot the thing. So do it.

It is, however, a good idea when sighting-in at home to shoot at closer and longer ranges just so you'll be able to check your scope at less or more than the standard 100 yards. In a caribou camp in Quebec the range was 48 yards long, and luckily I knew that my rifle should group 1 inch high at 50. This is about right for any high velocity center-fire sighted 3 inches high at 100 yards. But if you sight-in differently, shoot at closer ranges to find out just where your bullet lands.

And if you can, shoot at 200, 300, and 400 yards as well. The drop will not always match ballistics tables, and your 100-yard groups are not necessarily good indicators of long-range accuracy. Once I tested several rifles using Remington

Extended-Range ammo at 100 and 400 yards. All three rifles—a .280, 7mm magnum, and .30-06—produced three-shot groups of around ¾ inch at 100 yards. But at 400, only the .280 shot anything resembling a tight group, with several three-shot strings measuring about 6 inches or a little less. The two other rifles put three shots into 12 to 15 inches. Why? Some combination of bullet stabilization, scope parallax, and the whims of fate. Oh, and the drop varied from the ballistics tables by several inches in each case, partly because the velocity also varied, and partly because I was shooting at 6,500 feet above sea level.

For most big-game hunting, a good rule of thumb is to shoot no farther than the distance at which you can keep all your shots on a 9-inch paper plate—from field positions, not a benchrest. This is usually not as far as is claimed in many hunting stories, either published or told over a tin cup around the fire.

PART TWO

BINOCULARS AND
SPOTTING SCOPES

BINOCULARS: PORRO VS. ROOF PRISM

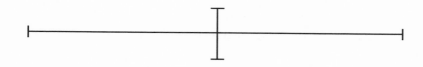

As Ortega y Gasset explained so simply and eloquently, the kill merely validates the hunt. It is not the hunt itself. Telescopic sights help us shoot with more certainty, but good binoculars *are* the hunt, the intense search that brings us to the mountains. I would rather hunt without a scope than without binoculars—and I often do, whether with bow or gun. Through binoculars we eavesdrop on the wild, bring animals and prairies and mountains almost inside us. If eyes are indeed the mirror of the soul, then binoculars can magnify our souls.

To me it is sad to see so many hunters without binoculars, or with cheap binoculars that distort the natural world. Whether in my backyard or remote Alaska, I feel almost naked without good binoculars because I know how much of the surrounding world exists beyond the vision (both literally and figuratively) of the average human. Binoculars almost provide another dimension to our planet, and even the heavens. My occasional pen pal Jeff Cooper calls the rifle the queen of firearms. I cannot help but feel that binoculars are the prince of the hunt.

But, you protest, really good binoculars are so damned expensive. How can an average hunter afford them? Well, so what? If you can afford a good hunting rifle and scope, you can afford a good binocular. It may take a few years to save the money, but I can show you how to buy a cheaper binocular that will do the job and last for those few years. If, like so many hunters, you have several rifles and a $50 binocular, then you're a fool.

Sharpness and brightness are the two biggest factors in evaluating the worth of binoculars. If a binocular doesn't possess them, it doesn't matter if it can withstand falling off a pickup hood, costs $1,000, or was made by German elves. Without the capacity to resolve details, a binocular is only so much metal and glass.

Today, more and more binoculars are providing a clear image thanks partly to computers. Before computers, binoculars were designed by engineers who ground and reground lenses according to the precepts of optics design and their slide rules. If the lab belonged to a top company such as Bausch & Lomb or Zeiss, enough time was spent that the binoculars turned out were as finely made as was humanly possible. If not, the binoculars produced would give those humans unlucky enough to peer through them a mule-kick headache within seventeen seconds.

Today, anybody with a computer and an optics program can design decent binoculars within hours. Time-consuming and expensive engineering is no longer as necessary. Consequently the optics of many inexpensive binoculars compare quite well with the best of thirty years ago. I have access to more than one optics lab, and tests show that some binoculars in the $250 range are just as sharp as binoculars

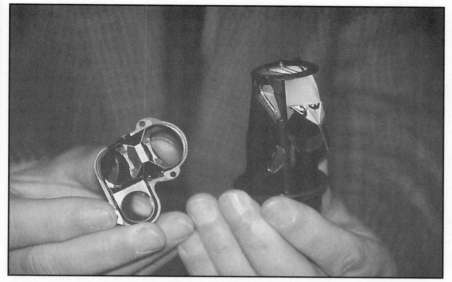

Here a Porro prism (left) and a roof prism (right) are shown removed from Zeiss binoculars.

costing three or four times as much. So why do some binoculars cost $250, some $500, and some $1,000?

One cliché in optics writing is that you get what you pay for. To a certain extent this is true. The very best binoculars will last much longer, and many expensive glasses provide the same optical quality as less expensive makes in a smaller, lighter package.

On the other hand, some big price tags have little to do with the quality of optics. As explained in the scope section, many European workers get paid much more than American or Japanese workers, and optics coming from overseas are slapped with an import duty. World economics has something to do with price, too. These days advances in manufacturing and optics occur so rapidly that they're hard to keep up with, in terms of both quality and cost.

At the moment, some of the old-time giants of the optics world are running scared, trying to keep ahead of the curve. For a long time German binoculars had the reputation of being the very best, and for a long time they were. Most of the twentieth century advances in binoculars were perfected in Germany, especially coated lenses and prisms.

But the rest of the world is catching up. With German wages among the highest in the world, they've been losing both technological superiority and market share. That's why Leica and Zeiss are building some of their stuff in America and other countries. Most of the other high-qual-

The two types of binoculars are the straight-barreled roof prism (top) and dogleg-barreled Porro prism (bottom).

ity optics firms from Japan and Austria are doing the same thing, and for the same reasons. As factories spring up in places like New Jersey, Portugal, and Thailand, prices drop. More importantly to hunters, prices for the same quality of optics drop.

All of this is changing so rapidly that I cannot say *this* is best or *that* is overpriced. What I will try to do is help you to tell good from mediocre from bad.

The main choices in binoculars come down to size (pocket, compact, standard, and huge) and prisms (Porro or roof). Since prisms have a lot to do with both size and money, let's look at those first.

Prisms don't exist in simple telescopes like riflescopes, in which the light passes straight through the scope from one lens to the next until it reaches your eyes. Because of this straight line of light, simple telescopes normally are pretty long.

A prism in the middle of a telescope "folds" the light in the middle of its passage, which means the telescope (or the pair of telescopes we call a binocular) can be shorter and often lighter. A 10X40 binocular, for instance, is much shorter than a 10X40 riflescope. (Some people also mistakenly use the term *field glasses*, which are not actually modern binoculars but a pair of simple, prism-less telescopes hitched together. These days, true field glasses are either toys or very long and heavy for their magnification— the reason we don't see field glasses in the field very often anymore.)

Modern binoculars use two prism systems: Porro and roof. Each has advantages and disadvantages.

Porro-prism binoculars use a pair of prisms that bend the light around two corners and, hence, have a dogleg shape to the barrels. Their advantages lie in ease of manufacture and a slight edge in sharpness over roof-prisms. Most optically good and less expensive binoculars are

Porro-prisms. They get their name from their inventor, an Italian named Ignazio Porro (1801-1875).

Roof-prism binoculars also use a pair of prisms in each barrel, but the light enters one end of the prisms and eventually emerges along the same line or very close to it. So roof-prism binoculars have straight barrels. They can provide the same optics in a smaller package, so an 8X40 roof-prism binocular is almost always more compact than an 8X40 Porro-prism.

But roof-prisms have an optical disadvantage. The light entering the prisms is split in half, right down the middle of the circle of light coming into the prism. It recombines before leaving the prism, but the light waves in each half of the view aren't aligned in exactly the same way. You might compare it to a placid stream with a rock in the middle. Above the rock the stream is smooth; below the rock the current is roiled.

This phase shift, as optical engineers call it, slightly softens the image in roof-prism binoculars. Until about a decade ago, all that could be done about it was make the binoculars as precise as possible.

But then some Zeiss engineers (who else?) figured out that coating the roof-prisms—in much the same way lenses are coated—reduced the phase shift and sharpened the image. Soon other top optics makers like Bausch & Lomb, Leica, and Swarovski figured out the same thing (probably by taking apart Zeiss binoculars). Soon all of the Big Four makers were phase-coating their best roof-prism binoculars. Known in optical slang as p-coating, this process essentially made roof-prism binoculars just as sharp as Porro-prism models of the same quality.

Until very recently p-coating was the province of the Big Four, but both Pentax and Nikon have now figured it out. They always made rugged, waterproof roof-prism binoculars that weren't quite in the same optical league as the

Europeans, but that isn't true anymore. The latest p-coated roof-prism binoculars from Pentax and Nikon are not only optically very fine, they're actually better than some of the equivalent European models.

Consequently, the price of superb roof-prism binoculars is starting to drop like a rock. You can buy the incredibly sharp and bright 8X42 Pentax DCFs for under $500, as compared to a minimum of $750 for the equivalent from the Big Four. No wonder the old-time firms are nervous. We're going to see a

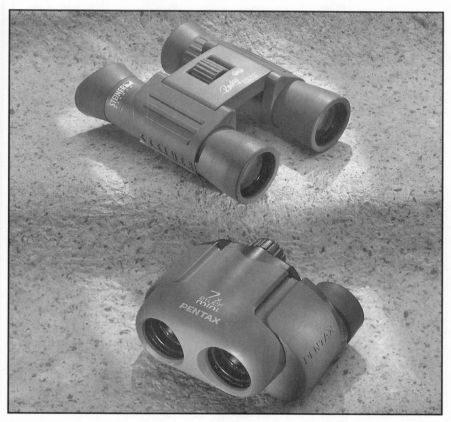

In compact binoculars the roof prism retains its typical form (top), though usually a plate rather than one long hinge is used to connect the two barrels. Compact Porro prisms (bottom) usually turn their dogleg barrels inward, with the objective lenses closer together.

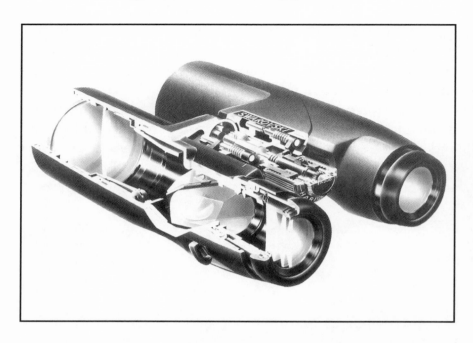

Cutaway views of roof- and Porro- prism binoculars show the different prism arrangements.

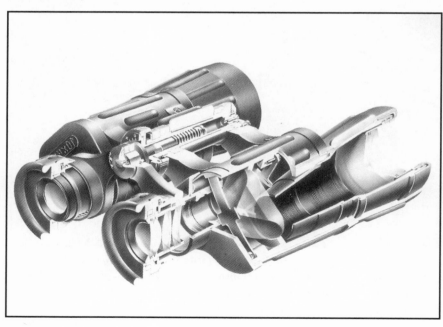

lot more shifting of manufacturing plants to countries with lower wage scales, so prices will probably continue to drop— if not quite so dramatically—over the next few years.

This amounts to nothing but good news for the hunter. An awful lot of very good but not quite first-class Japanese roof-prism binoculars are being imported right now under names from Burris to Weaver and selling for $300 to $400. Add p-coating for, maybe, $50, and they'll all be great. Normally, you have to pay at least $250 for optically good Porro-prism binoculars. Soon you may be able to have the advantages of roof-prisms for not much more.

As more companies p-coat their roof-prism binoculars, some companies will inevitably try to sell older, non-coated versions of the same binoculars as p-coated. There's a relatively simple test that will indicate if you're being conned. It requires two polarizing filters. The easiest way to get these is to buy a pair of the cheap sunglasses that clip onto regular glasses, then break the two lenses off.

Hold the binocular pointing toward a window with one of the lenses held over the eyepiece of one barrel. You can usually manage this with one hand; if not, tape the polarized lens so it covers the eyepiece. Now hold the other polarized lens in front of the same barrel's objective lens, and turn it back and forth, as if trying to twist the objective lens, while looking through that barrel of the binocular.

If the binocular's prisms are p-coated, the view will merely become slightly brighter and dimmer as you turn the polarized lens. If it isn't p-coated, half the view will become dark and the other half bright as you turn the lens, like the moon half in shadow and half in sunlight. This happens because light rays are aligned in the same direction in p-coated binoculars, but slightly out of alignment in uncoated binoculars.

I have read that Porro-prism binoculars are brighter than roof-prism models. Well, yes and no. One surface of a roof-prism functions as a mirror. In cheap roof-prisms, this mirror surface is backed by aluminum, which tends to absorb light. In quality binoculars, the surface is backed by silver or nothing at all, an optical trick made possible by a very long prism. Silver-backed and long prisms send much more light to your eye than do aluminum-backed prisms.

So low-priced roof-prism binoculars tend to be dimmer than equal-quality Porro-prisms. Top-line roof-prism binoculars tend to be brighter, simply because quality manufacturers tend to lavish the finest lenses and coatings on their best roof-prism models.

In full-size binoculars, roof-prisms also tend to be more rugged than Porro-prism models, everything else being equal. The roof-prisms themselves can be mounted more solidly inside the barrels, and the straight barrels of roof-prism binoculars also allow the use of a longer piano hinge rather than the long-armed hinges of most Porro-prisms. This tends to keep roof-prisms in collimation (alignment) over long periods of rough use.

An exception can be found in some compact models. Many compact Porro-prism models turn the dogleg of the barrels inward, with the objective lenses closer together than the eyepieces. This allows the use of a piano hinge, making them stronger than full-size Porro-prism binoculars. My friend John Flynn, local county attorney and elk guide, has a Porro-prism Nikon compact that's still in perfect collimation after more than a decade of hard use. (John probably wishes he could say the same about himself.)

Many pocket model roof prisms use two hinges, one on each barrel and connected by a plate; these can be folded up to fit in a shirt pocket. Two hinges are always weaker than one, but recently some one-hinge pocket-style roof prisms have appeared, notably the new Zeiss models, which tend to stay in alignment much longer than traditional two-hinge models.

But in full-size binoculars, the long piano hinge of roof prisms tends to keep binoculars in hunters' hands and out of repair departments. That's what you pay for in the very best binoculars: a lifetime of hard use. If you don't use your binocular all that much or under tough conditions, inexpensive models will last a long time and provide lots of great viewing. If you use them hard, however, they'll have to be replaced somewhere down the line. The top manufacturers have found that their new customers have usually owned two to four binoculars before stepping up. If you plan on long, hard use, it makes economic sense to buy the best first, if you can possibly afford it. It's far cheaper in the long run.

MAGNIFICATION, PRICE, & OTHER MATTERS

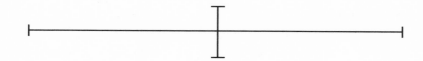

Most people think that magnification is the only virtue of binoculars. They rationalize that if they can buy 10X glasses for the same price as a 7X, they're way ahead of the game. First time binocular buyers also often choose pocket or compact models because they're both handier and cheaper. Hunters particularly fall for the camo-painted, rubber-armored roof-prism models we find stacked on sporting goods counters just before hunting season, usually priced around $49.95. Despite our connection to the wild, hunters are not much different from other modern Americans. Most of us are easy prey for any technology that claims to make our lives easier, and we are especially fond of such technology if it costs nearly nothing.

Small and inexpensive binoculars aren't totally worthless, but they bear little resemblance to the real thing. Almost any binocular helps us see better, but certain optical principles guarantee that small, cheap roof-prism binoculars will always remain a poor choice for serious hunting.

For one thing, it's more difficult to make small, precise lenses and prisms. Tiny binoculars suffer from such common ailments as doughnut view, in which the center of the view is sharp but the outside is warped or blurred. Combining low-quality, small objective lenses with cheap, aluminum backed roof-prisms will give you a view approximately as bright as a subway tunnel. As an optics-literate friend of mine once said after picking up a sample 8X20 on a sporting-goods counter and looking around the store: "They're dim, but they're fuzzy!"

Not incidentally, before the perfection of phase-coating, this problem applied even to expensive roof-prism compact binoculars. Back in 1987, I went to work for a Montana outfitter who had just been given, as a tip by a client, a genuine Zeiss binocular, the pocket-size 8X20 model. He wore these like an Olympic gold medal around his neck and couldn't believe it when I used my $200 8X40s to find a mule deer that he couldn't even see in a German binocular costing twice as much. We switched glasses, and only then did he find the buck.

The reason was quite simple. One basic optical principle (and one almost never written about in hunting magazines) is that bigger objective lenses not only gather more light but also improve resolution, contrast, and color rendition. This applies across the board, even in the very best binoculars. You will never be able to see the same amount of detail through the 10X25 Zeiss Design Selections as through the 10X56 Zeiss Night Owls. The difference will be most notable at dawn and dusk but also exists in the middle of the day.

The objective corollary is that, with a given objective size, less magnification means better resolution, contrast, and color rendition. A few years ago, a friend of mine who

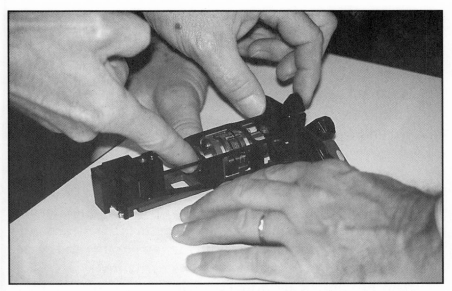

Here's the prism-floating mechanism of a 20X60 Zeiss stabilized binocular.

works for Swarovski called up and said the company was now making a 7X30 binocular exactly like its popular 8X30 except for the magnification. He'd just performed an experiment with the people in his office, taping over the model number on each binocular and asking for everybody's opinion. Eleven out of twelve people said the 7X had a slightly better view than the 8X: brighter, with better color and more detail. The twelfth called it a tie. I had been using a Swarovski 8X30 for several years for most of my timber hunting, but when my friend sent along a 7X30, I made the same comparison as the Swarovski office workers. I sold my 8X30s and now use the "weaker" version when I'm after deer and elk in the trees.

The same principle applies to the Zeiss 8X56 and 10X56 Night Owls. At a Zeiss seminar a few years ago, several of these were being passed around. Most people were pre-convinced that the 10X model had to be better, but Jim Carmichel, the world-famous gunwriter for *Outdoor Life*, didn't say anything immediately. Instead, he perched an 8X56 on top of a 10X56 and started looking through them alternately, comparing the view. "The eights are better," he said after a minute or so. We all tried the same trick and found out he was right.

The difference, of course, isn't much, but it is there. Given a choice between two binoculars that are exactly alike except for power, I'll take the lower magnification every time, because I'll be able to see more detail.

There is a limit to this, of course. You will not be able to see better out of a 4X30 binocular than an 8X30. That doesn't matter since nobody makes a 4X30. The manufacturers who make more than one binocular with the same frame and objective size change magnification 20 percent at most.

Another practical optical principle is that small imperfections in lenses and prisms don't affect, say, 8X40 binoculars the same way they affect 8X20s. Larger glasses may still suffer from doughnut view, but the clear center of the view will be larger, so you'll feel less eyestrain. In addition, the full-size binoculars will be a heck of a lot brighter. For serious hunting on a limited budget, I'd pick full-size Porro-prisms of around 7X35 or 8X40. As this is written in 1998, you can buy very decent Porro-prism binoculars of this size for not much more than $100, and $200 to $300 will buy optics almost as fine as any made. Look at the good Japanese brands like Fujinon, Nikon, and Pentax, or American brand names such as Burris, Leupold, and Simmons that import good Pacific Rim Porro-prism binoculars.

But if you're a woods hunter, or for any other reason feel you really need compact binoculars, these can be a great bargain, usually costing half to two-thirds the price of full-size binoculars of comparable quality. As this is written, even the very finest compacts retail for less than $400.

In the mid-price range, say from $200 to $300, all the top Pacific Rim manufacturers make solid Porro-prism compacts, but any of these big enough for real hunting will not fit in your pocket. For true hunting quality "pocket" binoculars, not tiny toys, the choice still comes down to roof-prisms. I haven't found any roof-prism pocket binoculars under around $350 that are worth a damn, but for that price or a little more you can buy Leicas, Swarovskis, and Zeisses, all of which are superb. (This price will probably drop as more Japanese companies start phase-coating their pocket models.)

However, the laws of optics aren't suspended here. While all the above firms offer compact models of at least 10X, less is more. For instance, the 6X18 Zeiss Design Selection is noticeably brighter than Zeiss's 8X20 and 10X25 pocket models, and just as sharp.

At the other end of the scale, there are some very good 10X40 binoculars around, but with 40mm objective lenses you'll often be better off with 8X binoculars. In truth, I regard 10X (and the increasingly common 12X) as specialized magnifications. To really outperform 8X glasses, 10s need 50mm lenses. In full-size glasses, the largest part of a binocular's weight comes from the objective lenses, and 10X50s and 12X50s are quite simply too much binocular to carry around on your neck all day.

Yes, there are various aftermarket doodads that redistribute the weight of big binoculars and make them more tolerable. Most involve some sort of additional strapping that goes around your back and shoulders, which does prevent neckstrain; however, they're a pain to take on and off, and no matter how comfortable you make big binoculars, they're bulky. Shooting from a prone position is an impossibility with a 10X50 strapped to your chest, and even shooting from the sitting position can be a problem. If you're bowhunting, the problem's even worse.

You can carry big binoculars with a cross-shoulder carry like many African professional hunters use, with the strap

The 20X60 stabilized Zeiss is a heavy handful and, at around $5,000, a wallet-ful as well. But it allows hand-held viewing at astonishing distances.

lengthened to go over one shoulder, the binocular riding on the opposite hip. But African PHs normally have one or two people to carry their other stuff. When hunting here in Montana I have noticed a general lack of gunbearers, and elsewhere in North America even highly paid outfitters rarely provide an extra teenager to carry your lunch.

So I normally have a daypack and a rifle strapped to myself, which makes the cross-shoulder carry less than practical, though it does work wonderfully for birdwatching. When I feel a real desire for a binocular bigger than an 8X40, such as when glassing the high plains of eastern Montana and Wyoming for mule deer, I typically wear a compact to midsize binocular around my neck and tote the big boomer in my pack. Serious glassing demands that you spend as much time sitting as hiking anyway, so that's what I do—sit down and haul out the heavy artillery. The smaller binocular works fine for the stalk, once something's spotted.

MAGNIFICATION, PRICE, & OTHER MATTERS

Here's where we get into a discussion of sheer weight, a rarely discussed feature of binoculars. Before getting into specifics, let me say that I firmly believe general hunting binoculars should be carried around your neck, ready to use. Amateur glassers tend to carry them in their daypack—with the binocular often still in its case, complete with those flimsy plastic lens covers provided by the factory. When these hunters think they see something across a big draw, they have to take off their pack, rummage for the binocular case, take out their 8X42, remove the lens covers (carefully placing them in the case so they won't get lost), readjust the eye spacing and focus, and then try to find that strange-looking branch they saw five minutes ago.

If you are one of these people—you're losing 99 percent of the use of your binocular. If you prefer not to be shot by your guide on some Big Trip Out West, here are some rules to live by. Number One: Throw away the lens covers for your binoculars, unless a one-piece slip-off cover for the rear lenses is provided. These normally attach to the straps, and come in handy in rain or snow. Number Two: Leave your case back at the motel or in camp. It's fine for transporting binoculars, but not for hunting. Number Three. Adjust your strap until it's comfortable. I like a short strap, just barely long enough to get the glasses over my head. That way they don't bounce around when I'm walking, or rattle around on my knees when I bend over to tie my bootlaces. But do whatever works, or feels right, just so long as you have the things around your neck when the guide whispers, "Lookit that elk!"

For binoculars to live around your neck, they can't weigh too much. I cannot speak for everybody, but over the years I have noticed that binoculars of twenty-four ounces (1½ pounds) or under are much more tolerable over a long day, and especially a long week, than anything heavier. About the most I can take for serious all-day hunting is thirty-two ounces, and even that can get annoying after several days.

You will not find any 10X50s in this range. At the lower end will be binoculars with 30–36mm objectives, at the upper end glasses with 40–42mm objectives. So in the lower end I generally use 7X, in the upper 8X. All my binoculars of 10X or 12X have 50mm or larger lenses, or larger objectives. They're the ones that go in the daypack, while I wear a smaller binocular around my neck.

Speaking of heavy binoculars, right here I'd like to talk about the military surplus binoculars that have been coming onto the market in recent years. A lot of these are advertised as being made in former Zeiss plants or other high-quality facilities. This is true, but even if made in the 1980s they were made with the technology of fifty years ago.

As the Soviet Union took over Eastern Europe, almost all optical advancement essentially stopped. The Soviet military instead poured its research money into rockets, aircraft, and other weaponry. In fact, many of the newly manufactured binoculars made in Eastern Europe (and even some binoculars and scopes being made today elsewhere in Europe) are still being made with World War II technology.

Though the Eastern Europe and Soviet military surplus binoculars on the market are optically quite good for their era, the examples I've seen have all been very heavy. The view is usually sharp, but it's often marred by yellow filters, or military reticles that have no use in hunting and serve only to clutter up the view. If roof-prism binoculars, they're surely not phase-coated. Most of the stuff I've seen advertised costs from $300 to $500. For that much money you can buy one of today's binoculars that's a lot lighter, optically finer, and just as rugged.

Some of you may also be wondering why zoom binoculars aren't more common, given the popularity of variable scopes. There are some on the market, but they haven't sold too well, and for several excellent reasons.

MAGNIFICATION, PRICE, & OTHER MATTERS

First and foremost is that the really useful magnification range for hand-held binoculars is pretty small. About 6X is the minimum needed for viewing distant objects—and as I've noted, 6X is poison on the market, and these days 7X is just barely acceptable. At the top end, 10X to 12X is about all most of can usefully hold in our hands. More than that and we lose image quality to vibration, and might as well be using less magnification.

To make higher power, say 15X, truly useful, you need at least 60mm objective lenses. This means a binocular far too large and heavy for general use. Moreover, hunters (and birdwatchers) want waterproof binoculars these days. It's tough enough making waterproof binoculars without adding the extra moving parts needed for variable magnification.

The truly salable and useful magnification range of any variable binoculars, therefore, would be about 7–10X. That isn't a lot of difference. While the variables on the market have much larger ranges, often as much as 7–15X, they don't sell particularly well because they don't appeal to the two main binocular-buying groups. These include the casual user who wants the cheapest possible glass, and the serious birdwatcher or hunter who needs the best available. Since variable binoculars don't sell well, the manufacturers don't waste extra engineering in their design or fine materials in their construction. (This is a long-winded and indirect way of saying variable binoculars aren't the best optically.)

The good-to-excellent, high-magnification (above 12X) binoculars on the market are all fixed-power models, and really specialized. With a couple of exceptions, they need to be mounted on a tripod. If they aren't, you lose more image to vibration than you gain through magnification.

Binoculars of 15X and up are essentially used as spotting scopes, and, indeed, most feature tripod threading in the front of the center-focus bar (as do many other glasses

Here are three 8X binoculars, clearly showing the different exit pupil size inherent in smaller and larger objective lenses. From top, a 8X20 Zeiss, 8X42 Pentax, and 8X56 Swarovski.

of 10X or even less). Though big binoculars have less magnification than most spotting scopes, the stereoscopic effect of binoculars provides more detail—and more comfortable glassing—than the monocular vision of a spotting scope. You can usually see as much or more through a good binocular of about 15X as through a 20X or even 25X spotting scope.

There aren't many really good, big binoculars on the market, but because of the relative ease of building bigger lenses, there are some real bargains. Pentax makes 16X and 20X glasses that retail for around $200. Because they both feature 50mm objectives, the 16X model is brighter and sharper—amazingly so, and totally usable for tripod-style glassing. On the other hand, the 15X60 Steiners I've seen have all suffered from severe doughnut vision. If you can afford the $1,500 price tag for something like the 15X60 Zeiss, the best glasses in this magnification range are of course sharper and brighter than the lower-priced brands.

The exceptions to the rule that anything above 12X must be hand-held are the image-stabilizing binoculars from Canon and Zeiss. They work on two principles. The Canon uses prisms that in effect change shape as the binocular moves, while Zeiss suspends its prisms in a mechanical system that works like multidimensional shock absorbers.

Though the systems differ, the result is remarkably similar. Instead of an image that bounces during every twitch, breath, and heartbeat of your body, it's as if you're standing on the deck of a rolling ship, watching a very steady island. If you sit down and rest your elbows on your knees, all image shake disappears. You can literally hold either binocular with one hand and see detail perfectly at 15X or 20X.

But as in the rest of the optical world, there is no free lunch. The 20X60 S Zeiss is more powerful, but at over 3½ pounds it's also huge. While the optics are, of course, superb, real world price is almost $5,000. The three IS (Image Stabilizing) Canon models—a 10X30, 12X36, and 15X45—cost a lot less, retailing for about $1,000 to $1,500 and weighing 21 to 36 ounces. The optics are very good, too.

So what's the problem? You'll note that all four binoculars have only 3mm exit pupils. Because of this the Canons simply can't compete in brightness with such standard models as the 10X42 Pentax, 12X50 Leica, or 15X60 Zeiss, revealing a severe lack of contrast, definition, and color in dim light. The big Zeiss gets away with a tiny exit pupil because of its incredible lenses and high twilight factor. Consequently it's the only one of the four that provides a real advantage over standard binoculars, and that only for very specialized hunting. If I were a Stone-sheep guide charging $15,000 a hunt, I'd probably own a 20X60 S. Swarovski used to make a huge 30X binocular, but you needed your own banker and Sherpa to carry the loan and the load.

Before moving on to spotting scopes—for most of us a far more practical solution to really long-range viewing—let us review the basics of binocular magnification versus price and portability:

1) Thou shalt not purchase cheap roof-prism binoculars, or your vision shall be forever blighted by doughnuts and your frontal lobe by headaches.

2) The best immediate bargains in all the binocular kingdom are full-size Porro-prism binoculars. These can be had for anything from $100 up, and in the $250 price range will often provide optics equal to the finest $1,000 European roof-prisms. But in general they will not last as long.

3) Good compact Porro-prism binoculars and mid-price (which means without phase-correction coating), full-size roof-prism binoculars will not provide quite the same optical brightness and sharpness as full-size Porro-prism

binoculars, but will normally last much longer due to their hinge design and solidly mounted prisms.

4) The best phase-coated roof-prism binoculars are the finest long-term purchase, whether you're buying compacts or full-size glasses. They will be rugged enough to pass down to your grandchildren, barring theft, an avalanche, or being left on the ground around pack mules. They will be small enough to carry around the hills and optically as good as any binoculars made. Luckily, these days you can buy top-grade, waterproof roof-prism binoculars for around $500, which makes the choice for the serious hunter that much easier.

TESTING FOR
QUALITY

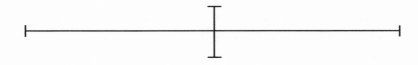

Since you now know the basics of binocular design, let me outline a few ways to tell good binoculars from bad. I could just write a long list of the worst to best models I've ever tested, but that would be subjective to a certain extent, and a total waste of time in two or three years after 163 new models will have come onto the market. Binocular technology is changing much faster than riflescope technology.

The basics of testing binoculars yourself are pretty easy. First, look through them, then extend your arms until you can see in each rear lens our old friend, the exit pupil. Is each exit pupil perfectly round or flattened on one or more sides? If flattened, it usually means the prisms are made of low-cost glass, so the light refracts off the sides of the prism, screwing up the whole optical system. This happens when the manufacturer uses cheap materials. Some flattening can also occur simply because the binocular's interior optics are slightly out of line.

Binoculars with squared exit pupils usually suffer from the doughnut vision mentioned earlier, with the view fairly sharp in the middle but fuzzy toward the edges. These can fool you for a moment, especially with full-size glasses, because your eye is naturally led to the middle of the field of view where everything's sharpest. After a few minutes of serious glassing, you'll notice your eyes getting tired. They keep trying to focus the whole view and not succeeding, so if you see any squaring of the exit pupils, pass.

Next, look through the binocular for more than a quick glance. To do this realistically, you must focus the thing. I've heard a lot of people complain they can't focus binoculars, but that's usually because they've been using cheap glasses that can't be focused for anyone.

Most binoculars have two adjustments, a center lever or dial that focuses both barrels at once, and a diopter adjustment (usually on the right eyepiece but often found on the center post) that allows for the slight differences between our eyes. Look for a diopter that, once set, stays there. There's nothing more annoying than having to reset the diopter every time you raise the binocular. For the same reason, many hunters prefer dial rather than lever center-focusing; the lever gets pushed out of whack too often.

The diopter setting has a mark indicating the center, with a plus sign on one side and a minus sign on the other. Set the diopter on the center mark and look through the binocular, then focus, using the main focusing lever or wheel. Setting the diopter in its central position means both barrels are focused exactly the same, and, unless your right and left eyes are very different, that setting should be pretty close for most people, especially if you wear corrective lenses.

I've read about many fancy ways to adjust diopters, which have probably scared some people away. Just keep looking through the binocular while twisting the diopter slightly. Turn it back and forth until the strain goes away.

You may have to tweak the center focus again slightly, but normally a slight adjustment of the diopter brings everything into focus. If it doesn't, then either something is very wrong with the binocular (common) or your eyes are widely different (uncommon, but possible).

Some binoculars use individually adjustable eyepieces. With these, each eyepiece is turned until it focuses for that eye. Many use clicks to keep the adjustments precise and in place. Their only disadvantage lies in quick looks at short distances—the reason birdwatchers don't like them—but for all except deep-woods hunting they work fine.

Many hunters ask about focus-free binoculars. These are actually fixed-focus glasses, and they work through the adaptability of our eyes. Instead of you manually focusing the binocular, your eyes adjust to the binocular. Fixed-focus binoculars are designed for people with 20/20 vision in both eyes. For those rare souls, they do work.

Unfortunately, most of us have eyes whose vision varies slightly, even when corrected by glasses or contact lenses. Or both eyes are slightly imperfect. For us, fixed-focus binoculars work for a few seconds—until our eyes get tired. And none of the fixed-focus binoculars on the market are of more than mediocre quality. For serious glassing, you need binoculars that focus.

Now that the binocular is focused, look through it again for just a few seconds. Feel a "pull" in your eyes? If everything's in focus, this pull is normally caused by the binocular being out of collimation, a technical term meaning alignment. To check for bad collimation, look through the binocular at some object at least 100 yards away, such as a stop sign. Holding the binocular as level as possible, first close your right eye and then your left, alternately. The stop sign should remain in very nearly the same place, no matter which eye you look through. If the image "hops" very noticeably right and left as you alternately close your eyes, then the binocular is out of vertical collimation, meaning that one barrel points to the left or right of the other.

Be aware, however, that many binoculars slightly "cross." That is, the image through the right barrel is slightly to the left of the image from the left barrel. There's a reason for this: Our eyes are slightly crossed most of the time. They have to be in order for both eyes to be pointing at the same object, especially the hamburger on our plate. The eyes of most people can't diverge or uncross, so the two barrels of binoculars cross slightly to accommodate our normal vision.

Next, hold the binocular a few inches from your eyes and look at some horizontal line, such as a street curb. The field of view will, of course, be much smaller, but you should still be able to see the curb in each ocular lens. It should be at the same level in each barrel. If not, the binocular is out of horizontal collimation, which means that one barrel points higher than the other.

Sometimes, of course, binoculars will be out of collimation both vertically and horizontally. The technical term for this condition is POS, an acronym for a "piece of something."

Squared prisms, the inability to focus for your eyes, and misalignment are automatic outs. But if the binocular passes all three of those tests, test sharpness and brightness. Unless you've looked through dozens of binoculars (in which case you probably aren't reading this), compare several binoculars at a time because brightness and sharpness are relative. One day when we were comparing a pile of binoculars, Bill McRae handed me his latest invention, a couple of toilet-paper tubes taped together. Then he urged me to look into his neighbor's open garage. Wow! Things sure brightened up! The reason? Looking through a tube shuts out peripheral light, forcing the pupils of our eyes to expand. To make any true brightness comparison, you must compare specific binoculars, side by side.

If you're inside, don't look out a window. Everybody does, almost automatically, but that's the worst test for brightness and sharpness. The view through almost any binocular looks pretty good when you peer from the dim interior of a sporting-goods store into a sunlit street. The pupils of your eyes shrink because of the bright light. This sharpens your vision, just like changing the f-stop on a camera lens sharpens the image. You won't be able to tell the difference in brightness between tiny compacts and huge night binoculars.

Instead, look into the dimmest recesses of the store and try to read the labels on boxes. This will quickly separate the bad binoculars from the mediocre from the really

Jim Carmichel demonstrates his highly technical binocular-testing method. This is the best way to compare two similar binoculars for brightness and definition.

good. Once you've pared the list down, stack one binocular on top of the other and look through them alternately. If you look quickly between them, at license plates and into dark corners, you'll soon be able to perceive the differences between good and great.

Next, check for mechanical quality. Does the focus adjustment work quickly, without slack or hard pushing? For really serious glassing I like to wear a baseball-style cap and grab the bill along with the binocular. I have met several guides who do the same thing. This really steadies the view, but the new roof-prism binoculars from Leupold have a center-focus wheel that turns easily under this pressure, mostly due to its location on top of the right barrel. This doesn't sound like much, but everything adds up when you live with a binocular day after day.

Some binoculars have such nicely fitted adjustments that freezing water will quite literally lock up the binocular. This can happen in the field, especially when hunting in wet snow. Look for a little clearance around the focus wheel.

Do you wear eyeglasses? If so, rubber eyecups on binocs should fold back and stay there, without developing any telltale cracks. Up to a certain point, money pays for a lifetime of use. I've seen the eyepieces on cheap binoculars fall off in one hunting season. Wiping them with the same antioxidant you use on the tires of your pickup slows this deterioration down. When exposed to long hours of sun, all but the very finest rubber will eventually fall apart anyway.

That's the reason many manufacturers are switching to sliding or screw-mounted eyecups, rather than folding rubber. These cost more, of course, but are worth it if you wear glasses and intend to use your hunting binoculars hard. Screw-mounted eyecups also provide adjustable eye relief. Rubber cups are either folded or extended out, which means you have no real choice if your own eye relief falls somewhere between.

Some binoculars feature very long eye relief. Just as in scopes, this reduces field of view. I've found an extra wide field even more overrated in binoculars than in scopes. If you wear glasses when hunting, as I usually do, long eye relief can often make binoculars usable even without folding down the eyecups. (Incidentally, until I started wearing contact lenses for some wet-weather hunting, I had no idea that your own face could fog binoculars. There are some advantages to eyeglasses in hunting, including eye protection.)

Unless you hunt only in a dry climate such as the arid West, you should probably buy waterproof binoculars. A decade ago these were pretty rare, but more and more waterproof models are being made these days. Why should we use fog-proof scopes while the view through our binocular looks like a bad day in Seattle? I've even had binoculars fog in Montana when snowflakes landed on the right eyepiece and melted due to my body heat. The water oozed inside the binocular, fogging that barrel. An overnight rest next to the woodstove dried everything out, but why bother? Buy waterproof.

The question, however, is what constitutes waterproof. To be waterproof under the tons of pressure 100 feet underwater, a binocular would have to weigh several pounds. But most of us merely ask that our 8X40s remain clear after a week of hunting in the rain. If you really need waterproof glasses, buy only those that advertise the fact, then dunk them in a sink full of warm water when you get home, as described in chapter 2. Let them cool off, then freeze them for a few hours and dunk them again. If bubbles pour out, send 'em back.

Be aware that it's harder to keep binoculars waterproof than scopes, simply because there are more moving parts than in scopes. Swarovskis are supposedly waterproof, and no new Swarovski binocular I've dunked has ever leaked. But I have lost count of the guides and serious hunters I've talked to who bought Swarovskis and eventually had them fog. Of course, Swarovskis have a lifetime guarantee, and the company will back it up, but it's hard to send binoculars back to the factory while in the middle of a brown bear hunt in Alaska.

One guide in British Columbia has gone to the new Leupold roof prisms, which aren't phase-correction coated (though they will be soon, or so I am told) and so aren't quite so bright and sharp as Swarovskis or other top-line roof prisms. But they don't fog. Evidently Leupold's experience in making absolutely waterproof rifle scopes has carried over into binocular manufacture as well.

The last, but by no means least, factor is feel. If you glass seriously, the binocular you choose will be in your hands for hours each day. Some just feel right and others don't. Luckily, more manufacturers look at ergonomic design these days, and it's really rare to find a binocular that feels totally clumsy.

But there are subtle differences. Right now I have two 12X binoculars in my collection, a 12X56 Simmons and a 12X Leica. Though the suggested retail price of the Simmons is only about a third of the Leicas, they're actually very good optically—though obviously not as good as the Leicas—and ¾ of a pound lighter. Despite the light weight, however, it simply doesn't feel as comfortable in my hands. Balance has a lot to do with this. The Simmons feels "muzzle heavy," if I can borrow a shooting term, with too much weight up front. The Leica, despite weighing more, balances perfectly and is much more comfortable for long-term looking.

Other differences can make or break a hunter's choice. I know one guy who rejected Leupold's fine little 7X30 Wind

River Porro prism because the strap slots are underneath the barrels rather than on the side, the common arrangement. When he hung the binocular around his neck, it tilted outward from his chest, and he didn't like that. My advice is to put the strap on and see how it feels. You can buy aftermarket straps to replace the quarter-inch straps many manufacturers provide, but a decent factory strap makes life easier.

CHOOSING A
SPOTTING SCOPE

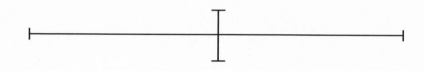

Perhaps it's the prejudice of a native of the wide-open spaces, but I believe every big-game hunter should own a spotting scope. Scopes help spot bullet holes in targets, allow you to scout white-tailed deer from a mile across Farmer Jones's field, and let you know whether that distant pronghorn buck has large horns. Among other things, I've used spotting scopes to look at Rocky Mountain tanagers in full breeding plumage and gaze at the moons of Jupiter. These last have nothing to do with chasing game, but many of the pleasures of hunting do not.

Life is better with a spotting scope, no matter where you hunt. Exactly which scope is another question. Almost any spotting scope on the market is better than none at all. If at least 20X, a good scope will show you things unseeable with a 10X binocular. If you'll use your scope merely to spot bullet holes while sighting-in, then an affordable scope will serve about as well as any. If you plan on hunting, spend more.

Most spotting scopes use the same Porro or roof prisms of binoculars, but the Leupold 12-40X60mm uses a mirror system. Johnny Unser glasses a big Alaskan valley for caribou.

My friend Corey Huebner, a back-country mule deer nut, once purchased a $100 scope that had pretty sharp optics. He frequently patted himself on the back for finding such a bargain—until the day he hiked into the Missouri Breaks and heard the musical notes of loose glass coming from his daypack. After riding on Corey's back and in his pickup for hundreds of rough miles, one of the interior lenses was rattling around inside his bargain.

But really good spotting scopes don't cost as much as really good binoculars, or even riflescopes. Spotting scopes don't need reticles, or to be in collimation. Fixed power of around 20–25X will do 75 percent of what any hunter needs, and a quality scope of about that magnification provides more value than a variable in the same price range. So if budget is a real factor, look at fixed scopes.

Variable spotting scopes do possess very real advantages; however, these are sometimes limited in actual field use. Some variables range up to 60X, but rarely is more than 40X usable in the hunting field, and then only on days (or during hours) without significant mirage. Air is really still only at dawn and dusk. Even in cold weather sunlight will cause ground mirage, not a product of desert heat but of different air densities. The full sun on a frozen mule deer mountain will send waves of lightly heated air curling across your view, obscuring entire herds of distant deer.

In addition, more magnification means a smaller exit pupil. Most hunting scopes have objective lenses of 50mm or 60mm. Even a 60mm objective means that at 20X the exit pupil is only 3mm, about the same size as most 7X compact binoculars. At 40X the exit pupil shrinks to 1.5mm, which turns things very dim. Though a deer across a shadowed canyon may look larger at 40X, you'll be able to see it far better through the same scope at 20X.

So high-power variables suffer at both midday and dusk from the demons of small exit pupils and midday mirage. In practical terms 40X is all that's usable in the field, and that only occasionally. Variable models topping out at 35X to 45X are probably the best all-round scopes, since they're also much smaller and lighter than variables that go up to 50X or 60X.

Because variables can be turned up and down, they can be adjusted to changing conditions of light and mirage, prob-ably their biggest advantage over fixed-power spotters. You can also turn a variable down to 12X or 15X for a wider field of view, find a distant deer, then zoom in for a closer look. The smaller field of a fixed 25X scope makes this tougher.

As with binoculars, Porro-prism scopes have an inher-ent optical advantage over roof-prism scopes, being slightly sharper—unless the roof-prism is phase-coated. There are a few "p-coated" scopes on the market, and because of the roof-prism they are slightly more compact than Porro-prism models. But since spotting scopes don't normally come in pairs, the roof prism's advantage in size isn't nearly as great. So far more companies make top grade Porro-prism spotting scopes than great Porro-prism binoculars.

(I must also point out that roof-prism scopes not p-coated are inferior only when we use the whole view. The softening of the image is caused by merging the two halves of the split roof-prism image. If you look through only one-half of the image—say the top half—there's no disadvantage to uncoated roof-prisms. Some people do this, probably those with split personalities.)

A few spotting scopes don't use prisms at all, and some literally "do it with mirrors." The oldest, non-prismatic design is the drawtube scope, like the traditional hand-held scopes favored by red stag hunters in Scotland. In their simplest forms these function as straight-line telescopes (exactly like a riflescope), and when folded up they're compact. But at full length they are too awkward for most hunting uses, and the design—essentially a piston inside a cylinder—tends to draw dust and moisture inside the tube. Consequently very few manufacturers bother with them anymore, especially for serious hunting scopes.

Swarovski, however, makes a couple of what it calls extendable telescopes with 75mm and 85mm objectives. These are thoroughly modern scopes that include roof-prisms in their design as well as a filter to keep out dust and moisture. But from what I gather, they have not set the world on fire, partly because they're big, heavy scopes even when folded up. The only one I've ever seen in the field was being wielded by a Swarovski representative in South Africa, and it never left the patio of the lodge.

Mirror scopes are another matter altogether. They can typically be made even shorter than prismatic scopes, especially the mirror lens scopes called catadioptric—or, more simply, cat. A cat scope features a concave objective with a small mirror in the center. Many astronomical telescopes as well as some photographic lenses use this design, and there was a minor fad of small cat scopes in hunting a few years back. It soon died, however, despite the small, packable scopes, and for a very simple reason: Their optics were garbage. Evidently it takes a lot of very precisely applied money to make a good, small cat scope, and it just never happened in hunting scopes. Come to think of it, I haven't seen too many mirror lenses in the hands of serious photographers, either, in recent years.

But the mirror system in Leupold's 12–40X spotting scope works very well indeed. It uses flat mirrors arranged on the same principle as a periscope, which accounts for the scope's boxy look but does result in a very short scope with sharp optics. It's also about as bright as any 60mm scope I've seen, waterproof, and comes in an ideal magnification range for hunting.

Many scopes can be purchased with an angled eyepiece so that you're looking down into the scope at a 45-degree angle when the barrel is level. Some hunters prefer these since they can be used more comfortably with a very short tripod. You lie on your stomach and look down as if viewing through a microscope. These are particularly handy when looking up at mountainsides above you, but when glassing from sitting, whether on the ground or from a vehicle, most hunters find them awkward. Moreover, since you're not looking directly at whatever you want to see, they also drive some people nuts. A very few scopes also come with rotating rear assemblies holding two eyepieces. With a twist of the wrist you can switch from a straight-line eyepiece to an angled one. But these aren't quite as rugged as standard scopes, and consequently not often used by serious hunters.

Most spotting scopes designed for hunting have objective lenses of 50mm or 60mm in diameter, an excellent compromise between portability and resolution. But for certain specialized purposes even more objective works better. In the past decade, a number of really big spotting scopes with objectives of 75–85mm have been introduced. These result in an exit pupil of around 4mm at 20X, which isn't bad even in an 8X binocular. It improves dim-light viewing spectacularly in a good spotting scope, especially since all the new super-spotters also use top-grade glass and lens coatings.

The first time I tested one of these big spotters was on a mountainside one November near my Montana home— the way I really prefer to test any hunting gear. A friend and I drove up a mountain road across a valley from a good elk ridge. The weather had been dry and warm, and under those conditions one of the best and easiest ways to take an elk is to glass during evening, then hunt those same parks the next morning. We used two good scopes with 50mm and 60mm objectives and a Bausch & Lomb Elite 20–60X77mm. And we found elk.

A small herd of five fed across a sagebrush park just as the sun touched the horizon. With the 50mm scope we could see they were elk, but only by color. We couldn't tell whether any had antlers, though if one had been a big bull the antlers probably would have been visible against the pale sage. With the 60mm scope we saw small antlers on the rear elk, but couldn't tell if they were big spikes or small "raghorns." But they were definitely antlers and not ears.

With the Bausch & Lomb we could see at least three or four points on each antler. This was uplifting because in southwestern Montana bulls must grow a brow tine to be legal. That ridge requires a tough hour to climb, and we wished to know if a shootable elk lived up there before making the effort.

As the sun went down, we had to turn the 50mm scope down to 15X; otherwise, the scene went almost completely blank. The 60mm worked at a maximum of 20X, while the 77mm scope still showed good contrast at 25X. The difference was there, and a very definite advantage.

But you pay for that advantage, beginning with price. A number of very good 60mm scopes can be purchased for $350 to $700. For the super-spotters from makers such as Bausch & Lomb, Kowa, Nikon, and Swarovski, you'll have to sacrifice that $1,000 bill you've been using as a bookmark, and maybe throw in a few hundreds as well.

You also pay in length and heft. Many smaller scopes aren't much bigger than a muscle-bound 3–10X riflescope, and even most larger 50mm or 60mm scopes will fit into one of the side pockets of my Polarfleece daypack. No 75mm to 85mm spotter will fit in the same pocket. Though none is too big to fit into the main bag of the same pack, I'd have to leave something else vital behind (lunch?) and carry more weight up the mountain. But for very specific uses, the bigger, brighter scopes have distinct advantages.

Compact Porro-prism spotting scopes are one of the bargains in optics. Canadian outfitter Pat Frederick uses a 10–30X Bushnell to scout for big Alberta deer.

Most big spotting scopes, and even many smaller models, come in one or more grades—the lower grades using standard achromatic lens systems. They are good scopes, but at high magnification even achromatic lenses show a faint line of color around the edges of objects.

The reason? At magnifications above about 15X it becomes increasingly difficult to bend all the different colors of the spectrum into our eye. So in many spotting scopes, one color or another doesn't focus in exactly the same way as the others. As a result you'll see a slight halo of color when focusing on some sharp-edged object such as a stop sign. Often the color will be purple or yellow, just a thin rim around the very edges of the object.

This halo cuts down on sharpness and contrast—qualities you bought a scope for in the first place—and is accentuated by higher power and bigger lenses. So most top manufacturers use apochromatic (fully color-corrected) lenses with extra-low dispersion (ED) glass or fluorite crystal in their very best scopes, and especially in their largest. These usually improve color rendition as well.

But all this sharpness and brightness is for naught if you can't hold the darn thing steady. Ah, yes, steadying the scope. It's essential to serious glassing, since the view through a bouncing or even vibrating scope is like glassing through falling rain. You lose the sharp edges of objects and are no better off than with a good binocular. One outfitter I know sometimes rests his spotting scope on his horse's saddle, as useless as typing with your toes. Yeah, you'll get letters on the page, but they won't mean anything.

A heavy camera tripod works better than anything, but few of us can afford tripod-bearers anymore. The Bogen I use for serious studio work weighs more than most .338s. It steadies the view, but I won't carry it farther than the 4-wheel-drive parked outside my front door.

CHOOSING A SPOTTING SCOPE

On timbered ridges you can sometimes attach a window mount to a branch—and window mounts also work, of course, on pickup windows. Some hunters use shoulder stocks, which work pretty well for sizing up a distant game animal that's already been spotted through binoculars. But in even the steadiest hands there's some quiver, and consequently the eye tires during long periods of serious glassing.

For most of the time, a compact tripod is the only practical solution. In anything less than a really stiff wind these work quite well. They grow steadier the lower they are to the ground. I like to lie on a ridge with the scope only a foot off the ground, but a tripod with enough height to allow you to sit is often useful.

Many people have trouble finding something with their new 25X scope. Spotting scopes have much smaller fields than binoculars, and finding a bedded mule deer that you've spotted across a basin with your 8X40s is often puzzling. Aside from turning a variable scope down to get a larger field, many scopes also feature a peep sight or low-magnification viewfinder for aiming. These are particularly useful on fixed-power models.

But you can still go nuts trying to show a deer to your partner. You watched through the scope while the buck stood up and stretched, but it's now bedded in the middle of a bunch of brown stumps. Leupold offers a practical option for this very problem: a cross hair in the spotting scope. Just aim it at the deer, and your partner can see what you see, but like blaze-orange handles on hunting knives, it is too practical for most of us. Leupold used to offer it straight from the factory, but nowadays you have to send your scope back in to be retrofitted.

Most scopes arrive rubber-armored these days, which protects the scope in backpacks or saddle bags without the hassle of a case. Optical quality is about the only other question, and you can use the same test as for binoculars. In a sporting-goods store or other indoor "testing facility," mount each scope on a tripod and turn it toward the dimmest end of the store. Fool with the magnification and focus rings, and see if the peep or aiming scope actually points toward the same place as the big scope. Check out the eye relief; some scopes work much better for eyeglass wearers. And if you're thinking about a variable, see if the scope remains focused as you run up and down the magnification range. This little feature isn't too common, even among good scopes, but helps enormously when you turn down to 15X in order to find a distant deer, then zoom in to 40X for a close look.

GLASSING

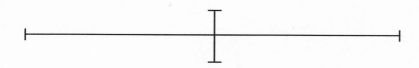

There are only three real "secrets" (that favored word of the hunting magazines) to improving your hunting success with binoculars. The most important is to wear your binocular, as you do your hunting coat. If it rides inside a daypack, you'll screw up Secret Number Two.

I've already mentioned Two, but you need to hear it more than once: Most hunters use binoculars to look at objects they've already seen with their eyes. Instead, a binocular should be used to find game you would not have seen with your unaided eyes.

Secret Three is to hold your binocular steady. You will not see much more detail through even the finest 10X binocular if the unit is shaking, twitching, or sweeping across the landscape like a broom. This is because only a very tiny particle of our eye really sees detail.

The macula is a dot in the rear of our eye, a tiny concentration of the color-seeing cones that transmit the world we see to our brain. The rest of our vision can detect motion, but doesn't see detail particularly well.

The macula covers only about 2 degrees of our vision— and when we magnify our vision with a binocular, we

African professional hunter Paul Stones glasses for kudu and anything else that might be found along the Limpopo River.

decrease that area proportionately. An 8X binocular, for instance, shrinks our area of sharp vision to about ¼ of a degree. We must have that fraction of a degree point steadily, right at the deer we hope to find, if we hope to see the deer at all.

When we "sweep" the landscape, all we'll see is the broadest kinds of motion—a running deer, for instance. We need to steady our binocular as much as possible in order to see the detail we bought the binocular for.

Those are the basics. Now let's apply them to the distances we hunt: close, middle, and long ranges. Examples of close ranges (woods) are white-tailed deer hunting in the oak forests of the East or still-hunting for elk in the lodgepole pine thickets of the West. Close-range hunting can be found anywhere game hides in timber or brush, like the thornbush country of Africa or the similar deer country in south Texas.

GLASSING

Here we're not talking about sitting down and looking over vast areas for hours. Instead we're normally still-hunting and sometimes stand-hunting—or a combination of the two, which is often what good still-hunting amounts to. We move slowly through the woods, trying to see game before it sees us, or very soon after it sees us. Or we sit in a ground blind or up in a tree stand and wait for game to come out to feed or drink or mate. Normally, any animal we see will be within rifle range.

This is where the hot-stove league says binoculars are useless. Why do you need a binocular to see a deer already in range? I will tell you something different, because I've found too many game animals with binoculars in thick vegetation, from a big bull kudu along South Africa's Limpopo River to a bull moose in an alder-covered Montana creek bottom.

The time I still remember best did not involve any big trophy or exotic locale. I was in college and needed cheap meat. The day before the opener of Montana's general big-game season, a friend in similar straits and I tent-camped in the mountains an hour west from Missoula, where we lived.

That part of the Rockies is not made up of wide-open spaces; instead, it's steep mountains and narrow valleys thickly timbered by larch, lodgepole, and Douglas fir. Unless you're looking across a clear-cut, you normally can't see one hundred yards, and often can't see twenty-five. But this country holds a variety of game, including mule and white-tailed deer, black bear, and elk. Any of the four were legal, and would have been sincerely welcome in our freezers.

It started to rain during the night. By the time we got up, the woods were soaked and very quiet, perfect still-hunting conditions. My friend hunted the canyon while I headed straight up the mountain beside us. A soft mist eased straight down in the still air.

About one thousand feet above our camp the air turned cool enough to change the rain to wet snowflakes. This is common in that part of the West, where after an early autumn storm the mountains often wear a cap of fresh snow.

Deer and elk know all about leaving their tracks in snow, the result of tens of thousands of years of being hunted. They often travel just below the snow line where their tracks are not nearly as noticeable. So I still-hunted one hundred feet or so below the snow line, contouring the mountain. The sodden brush under the trees, mostly snowberry and ninebark, remained silent as it slipped across my wool pants and jacket. I moved very slowly, covering perhaps ten yards a minute. At the edge of each little clearing I stood and looked hard for several minutes, first with my eyes so I wouldn't miss anything obvious, then with my 7X35 binocular, which had been purchased for $35 from Sears

On this day Jim Conley found Kodiak Island nice and sunny, but weather here can quickly change to dark and rainy. This is where truly waterproof binoculars are absolutely essential.

Roebuck. It had been made by an unknown Japanese firm that knew what it was doing, and worked just fine for a broke college student.

About an hour into my slow hunt I glassed something brown about fifty yards down the slope. Now, most of the world on that gray October day was varying shades of brown, but this something had a hint of white around one edge. My view was partially blocked by a branch, so I very slowly eased down on my haunches and looked again. The brown object was still there, a slightly different brown from the rest of the world. And then an ear flicked, and I could see a white-tailed deer bedded behind a rotting deadfall and looking downhill to my right.

It didn't matter what kind of deer it was—all were legal, does and bucks of both species—there wasn't anything to shoot at except part of the neck. I squatted there for a while until I realized my scent on this absolutely still day would soon ooze down the mountain and into the deer's nostrils.

So I raised my old Springfield .30-06 to my shoulder, my knees in my armpits. Though it is one of the handiest in close-range hunting, almost nobody ever writes about this is the amazingly steady squat position. It is much steadier than kneeling, and you can ease into it without sound. A squat also puts you below those eye-height branches that often block the human view to game, down where you can look "under" the woods to see deer and elk and all sorts of things. It works for both shooting and glassing.

The 3X Weaver scope on the '06 found the deer, and I shifted one foot just enough to make a sound. The deer's ears came up and its head turned, but it didn't move. I did see, however, that it was a white-tailed doe. Then I whistled as softly as possible, and the doe stood. The cross hairs found the shoulder, and the shot made a loud thud in the heavy moist air. The doe folded gently into its bed, right in its tracks. When I gutted her I found that the 200-grain Nosler had bored a clean hole through her shoulder, the top of her heart, and then went out through her last full rib.

That is the essence of using a binocular in the thick stuff. If you are really still-hunting instead of just walking through the woods, you should be trying to see game before it sees you. A good binocular is immeasurably useful in such hunting, even from a stand. With binoculars you'll be able to see if that slight flash of movement behind the oaks is a deer or a blue jay.

Even in the woods I tend to use smaller, full-size binoculars rather than compacts. They're so much brighter in the dim places deer and elk like to hide, but good compacts are far better than nothing at all.

One feature of binoculars that's rarely mentioned is their ability to separate layers of branches and leaves. Experienced hunters John Wootters and Finn Aagaard have noted this fact, and it derives, of course, from the limited depth of field of any hunting binocular at close range. At short distances in a woods, only a few feet of timber can be in focus, especially with binoculars above 8X.

This is why the few woods hunters who really use binoculars often prefer center-focus, rather than individual focus, which works perfectly well for any other sort of hunting. With center-focus you can slowly work your way through the nearby brush, often finding a deer in a "wall" of hard focus.

Far more likely you will find a part of a deer. This is another "secret" to any close-range hunting, even without binoculars. When still-hunting correctly, you'll almost never see a whole deer. Just what you do see is often something of a mystery. I have read that you should look for horizontal lines, since most tree trunks and branches are

The Missouri Breaks with a typical combination of rough-country optics: 7X35 binocular, compact spotting scope, and scope-sighted .30-06.

vertical or angled. In much timber there's deadfall everywhere, creating hundreds of horizontal lines. The white on various parts of mule deer, blacktails, and whitetails often shows up, and the flicking of an ear is a sure giveaway. Sometimes you'll see the black eyes (the "big brown eyes" of deer are so dark they appear black and as hard as obsidian when they are looking at you at any distance beyond a few feet) or the curve of an antler.

Elk should be the toughest to see since their coats match typical western timber more closely than that of deer or a nearly black bull moose. Even the buff-orange coat of a mature bull wapiti is almost exactly the same color as a barkless or broken conifer, common in much elk cover. On the other hand, a big bull's huge antlers will move a lot with the slightest twitch of his head, and elk tend to make noise, especially when in herds. So unless you have an advanced case of "shooter's disease" (usually called hearing impairment in these politically correct days), you'll hear the crackles, cow chirps, and belly rumbles of elk long before you see them. You should start glassing hard.

You also need to remember to bring your binocular up slowly. Any lifting motion is an alarm to the natural world. It means birds flying, squirrels scampering up a tree, deer rising from their beds. Other animals pick up on this signal, so bring your binocular up very slowly, and turn your head slowly.

In the woods, squatting is often the steadiest glassing position, but you can also help steady a binocular by wearing a baseball-style cap. By grabbing the bill of the cap between your fingers and the binocular, you have an anchor to steady your binocular. Things calm down amazingly. Combine this tactic with the squat, and you'll really be able to steady a binocular at close ranges.

Mid-range glassing is almost as rare as woods glassing. You almost never need a spotting scope at mid-ranges, but a full-size binocular of about 8X works great. Here we're talking about clear-cut woods or semi-open ridges, anywhere you can see up to about half a mile.

There's an awful lot of this sort of country in the West, but it can be found in other places, too. Late in autumn, after the leaves fall and the fields are harvested, you'll be able to see quite a way in the Midwest and even parts of the East and South. If you're hunting far enough north, snow on the ground provides a real advantage to somebody using a good, full-size binocular.

The reason? Snow makes deer much easier to see, but also makes you much easier to see. The Midwestern hunter who sits on any slight elevation, whether a tree stand or ridge, and glasses down into the whitened timber two hundred to eight hundred yards away is much more likely to see deer before they see him than any still-hunter, no matter how skilled. During the whitetail rut, it's amazing how many bucks you'll spot trotting along near the crest of an oak ridge, looking for love in all the white places.

The same technique works equally well across clear-cuts in the Rockies, even when there isn't any snow. Mule deer bucks like to bed up high, at the top end of a draw where they can see a long way but where there's some means of escape behind them. This precisely describes many clear-cuts in the West. If there aren't any deer out feeding along the edges of a clear-cut (and they dearly love the new browse that comes up for a few years after logging), glass the edges of the cut carefully. You may find a buck's white throat patch along the edges, or the Y of a mule deer's ears. Clear-cuts on National Forest land used to be too big to attract much game, but in the past twenty years or so smaller, ten- to forty-acre cuts have become the

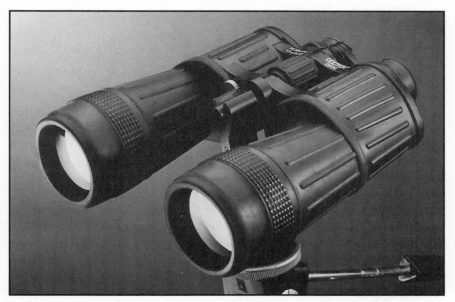

Many serious glassers prefer to use big binoculars—like this Docter 15X60B— mounted on tripods; consequently, many larger binoculars feature tripod threads in the front of their hinge.

norm, and are hotspots for deer and elk—as long as the logging road is closed. If there's no vehicle traffic, they're natural areas for a middle-distance glasser.

The big difference between real woods glassing and middle distances is that when looking from oak ridge to oak ridge or across lodgepole clear-cuts, you can sit down, put your back against a tree, and really pick apart the landscape. Spend more than a minute or two at the right time of year, and good things can happen. Of course, morning and evening are the best times, but during the rut, I've seen bucks moving at all times of day.

Here's a classic Western middle-distance glassing story. My wife needed a buck deer one November, so two hours before sundown we hiked up a wide coulee in the breaks along a big river. The south-facing slopes were covered with grama grass and occasional sage, while the north slopes held ponderosa pine and the occasional juniper.

Instead of trying to still-hunt the timber, which was dry, frozen, and as loud as dry pasta, we sat on a sandstone ledge and glassed. Just about the time the sun touched the tops of the trees along the ridge to the west, I saw a line of deer trot out of the timber, half a mile down the coulee. It was mid-November, the peak of the rut, and through the big, bright 10X50 Pentaxs I could see the antlers of a good buck silhouetted against the bright tan grass.

There wasn't much time, so we butt-skidded off the sandstone and hiked hard down the bottom of the draw, hidden from the herd. Eileen loaded the chamber of her .270 as we walked, then held it ready in the crook of her left arm. We approached the deer meadow from behind a finger-draw filled with pines, finally easing up behind a big ponderosa. The does heard the slight noise we made in the dry grass and pine cones, and were already suspicious when Eileen poked her .270 around the big tree. The lead doe started trotting off, not bouncing yet in that weird mule deer "stot," but definitely moving out. The other does started to follow, but the buck stood there looking our way, probably hoping we were another and even better-looking doe. Then the .270 cracked and the buck dropped, cleanly shot through both shoulders and the spine. Eileen did not want to be tracking a lung-shot deer under the trees after dark.

Long-distance glassing is in some ways the most relaxing way to hunt, if you have any patience. I have friends who simply cannot sit still for any length of time. If you can discipline yourself and buy the right optics, long-distance spot-and-stalking is not only relaxing but also provides one of the greatest thrills in hunting—the stalk.

Here you really plant yourself, almost as firmly as a tree, and look and look and look. This is where eye relief in binoculars becomes critical. Most of the time I don't worry about eye relief too much, as long as I can see most of the

Corey Huebner examines a clear-cut for black bear in northwestern Montana. This is classic mid-range glassing.

The author aims at a black bear at the bottom of a clearcut, while Sean Rising spots the shot with a 10X40 Bausch & Lomb. This is classic mid-range glassing in which, if you stop and look instead of taking a quick glance, you'll often find game along the timber edges.

field of view. In order for long-term glassing to be most comfortable, your eyes must be able to roam around inside the binocular.

The principle is pretty simple—akin to the fact that standing still for twenty minutes is much tougher than walking for twenty minutes. Similarly, our eyes grow tired when we have to stare straight ahead instead of looking around. Insufficient eye relief tends to force our eyes to look right down the middle of our binocular. Instead of letting our eyes do the walking around "inside" the field of view, we must hold our eyes steady and move the binocular.

To a certain extent, a small exit pupil forces the same sort of stiff viewing. While many compact binoculars have the optical quality for long-range glassing, their 3mm exit pupils just don't leave enough room for the eye to roam.

Over long periods of time both of these factors really make a difference. I like an exit pupil of at least 4mm and as much eye relief as I can get. Since I usually wear glasses when hunting, folding eyecups are absolutely necessary (lately I've come to prefer the telescoping or screw-in variety over folding rubber cups). Telescoping cups can be adjusted to exactly the right eye relief, while folding rubber cups provide only two settings: up or down. Sometimes neither is exactly right. While rubber-cup binocs are fine for relatively short-term glassing, they're a pain when you're looking for an hour or more.

Since this is very serious stuff, I often carry two binoculars and a spotting scope for open-country glassing. The two binoculars will usually be a lightweight (which does not necessarily mean a compact) model of around 7X or 8X and a bigger glass of 10X or more with at least a 50mm objective. For years, I used several 10X glasses from companies as varied as Bausch & Lomb, Leupold, and Pentax, but lately my favored big glass is the new 12X50 Leica. It's too heavy to carry around my neck but is compact enough to fit nicely in a daypack. The 12X magnification is the maximum I can handhold, and it "sees" noticeably farther than a 10X. Unfortunately, not many companies make truly great 12X binoculars; though with today's quest toward more magnification, expect more to show up.

After a deer is spotted, I either head off on the stalk with my smaller binocular around my neck or set up my spotting scope for a closer look. The trend these days for cutting-edge hunters is to use a great big binocular of 15X and up instead of a spotting scope. I have done this some myself, but generally prefer to combine my two binoculars with a good variable spotter topping out at around 35–40X. These aren't quite as good as big binoculars for actual spotting, but at really long distances of a mile or more they provide more detail than any 15X to 20X binocular, at least under ideal light conditions. They also cost a hell of a lot less than quality big binoculars.

Sometimes I also use them for glassing the really distant ridges. This normally creates some eyestrain after a half-hour or so, caused by squinting the off eye. I've solved that problem by taping the off lens of my glasses so I can glass with both eyes open. This really helps when glassing for an hour or more.

So you sit yourself down on a high point and look. The first rule of long-distance glassing is to look close first. A few years ago I was guiding a couple of guys after deer in the hills of eastern Montana and wanted to check out the head of a big draw. We drove close on a two-track road, then hiked up a little hill. I crawled to the top and started glassing while lying on my belly, elbows on the sand. I thought this would be a hint to my hunters. It was to one, who crawled up beside me, but the other walked right up to the top and stood there, glassing the far end of the draw almost a mile away.

The bedded herd of mule deer that I'd already spotted in the dry washout 250 yards below us didn't like this. There were five does and a medium-sized buck, and they climbed out of the wash and started away in that stiff-legged walk that says, "I am growing very nervous."

I whispered to my standing hunter, "You want that buck?"

"Where?" he barked excitedly. All the deer stopped and looked at us as if we'd spoken too loudly in a library.

"Right down there," I said, pointing.

"Oh, s---!" he said, rustling into a quick sitting position. "How far?"

"About 250 yards."

He aimed and aimed and aimed, and the does were starting off again by the time he touched off his .30-06. A puff of dust erupted over the buck's back, and they all left, stotting up the draw, over a fence, and onto a ranch where we could not hunt.

"Where'd you aim?" I said, knowing his '06 was sighted 3 inches high at 100 yards.

"Just over the back. I figured it'd drop that much at 250." This is perhaps the most common shooting mistake made by people visiting the open plains. They always want to "help" that bullet over those vast distances, even when they're already sighted-in for 250 yards.

Oh, well. We may have been able to sort that all out if both hunters had followed my example. We probably would have spotted the deer without them seeing us, and then had time to quietly discuss how to make the shot.

After looking close, you look medium, then long— you look a long time. Despite all the stories of finding a deer antler poking out from behind a rock, most often you'll find game by spotting movement of some sort. Once, on a big ridge in Alaska's Mulchatna drainage, we were glassing for caribou and also scouting for moose, getting ready for the season that would open two days later. We saw a few caribou, but none with big antlers. Then I saw something white directly across from us on a birch-covered ridge. I looked at it with my 10X40 Leupolds, then set up my spotting scope and looked again.

"There's a bull moose bedded over there," I said. The white was one of his antlers, freshly cleaned of velvet.

"Where?" the guide asked excitedly. My hunting partner, Gary Williams, turned to glass, too.

"Right over there, just below the highest point of that ridge, about one hundred yards to the right of that clearing just under the top." I looked again, and the bull was gone.

"Bulls---," said the guide, taking his binocular down and grinning. "You're hallucinating again." We'd gotten to know each other pretty well by then.

I shook my head and looked some more. Soon I saw some dark red right where I'd seen the bull. Then the white appeared again. "There he is. He just turned his head. His antler's still bloody underneath, so when he turns his head the other way, you can't see him through binoculars." And that was the case. The upper side of his antlers had been washed clean by a recent rain, but the underside was still covered by the burgundy of congealed blood. This may not have been the same 60-inch bull Gary killed almost a week later, but it was about the same size, and the undersides of Gary's bull's antlers were still much darker than the tops.

Alaskans talk of the flash of a bull moose's antlers in the sun, and that shiny headgear does indeed show up at remarkable distances. You also often first spot the whiter parts of many game animals, from the pure white of prong-horn rumps to the creamy necks of bull caribou to the dingy butt patches of bighorn sheep and mule deer.

In most country, there's usually something in nature that will look almost exactly like the animal you're glass-ing for. Black-bear country always seems to be covered with burned stumps, and mule deer and bighorn sheep country with gray-brown rocks. When I hunted javelina in Arizona, I was not surprised to discover that a barrel cactus in the morning light looks almost exactly like a desert pig, head down and feeding. And 99.9 percent of the time you'll look and look and discover you've been looking at a rock or stump or cactus. If you look long enough, eventually one will move.

Sometimes it's the light that moves. The sun comes out from behind a cloud, or the angle of the sun drops as sun-down nears. Suddenly you see an antler or horn that wasn't there before, but you've got to have those lenses pressed against your eyes to see this, and many people simply don't have the patience.

Or is it faith? Until you see how glassing works and find a distant buck or bear or bull and then stalk it successfully, most hunters simply doubt the whole process and give up too easily. They feel they're wasting time when they could be hiking the country.

Glassing in almost any country is the surest way to find yourself within short rifle or even bow range of game that's unaware any human is within half a mile. Once you've made a few of those final, easing stalks that bring you close, heart beating too palpably inside your chest, your knees and hands hurting with their contact with the earth, you'll find it very difficult to hunt without binoculars. In fact, you'll find it hard to enter the woods without them because it will feel as if you've left your eyes behind.

PART THREE

HIGH TECH
AND THE PAST

HIGH-TECH
RANGEFINDERS

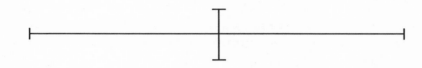

Humans have been estimating range since the day we first threw a rock at some animal. Back then we didn't guess in yards or even steps, but through practice. We threw until we knew how high and hard to throw at different distances, with different rocks. Even after the invention of the spear and atlatl, and then the bow and arrow, we estimated range the same way. With lots of practice, this technique still works.

Which is why today, centuries after the invention of the rifled barrel, most hunters guess at the range to a distant deer. Guessing doesn't work too well past atlatl range, which is the reason we have so many rangefinding reticles these days. (Chapter 6 also describes how to use a standard scope's reticle for distance estimation.)

Using a reticle to estimate distance, however, has one big problem. Even with the flattest-shooting modern rifles, you still need to know the size of the target within 10 percent. Even with familiar game animals, that isn't always possible. In new country it's often totally impractical.

With slower projectiles, such as arrows or blackpowder bullets, and at much closer ranges, critical range estimation becomes even more important. Even with the fastest overdraw compound bow, a pronghorn at forty yards is safe from someone aiming with the thirty-yard pin. A mule deer standing 150 yards away rather than the guesstimated 100 is totally safe from even the sabot bullet of most in-line muzzleloaders, which is why many hunters are starting to carry a high-tech rangefinder.

High-tech rangefinders don't require any knowledge of target size, but they do have disadvantages. A hunter must either carry an extra instrument or use a rangefinder incorporated into his binocular or scope. We shall also see that high-tech rangefinders are not infallible. Within their limits, however, split-image and laser rangefinders can be even more accurate than reticle subtension.

Split-image rangefinders work by triangulation. Most are tubes with a monocular at one end. Looking through the monocular, you'll see both a primary image (the normal view through the monocular) and a secondary image, reflected from a lens at the other end of the rangefinder. To find the range, the two images are merged in much the same technique you'd use to focus binoculars, and the distance is read from a dial.

A huge problem with split-image rangefinding is that accuracy is directly related to the distance between primary and secondary images. The military used split-image rangefinders for years. These are commonly at least four feet long; rangefinders of that size can accurately compute distances within five yards or so out to the practical limits of precise field riflery. Serious varmint shooters have used surplus military rangefinders for years. I once shot a groundhog field in West Virginia with my friend Melvin Forbes, and we used his ex-military split-image rangefinder, which accurately

Aside from accuracy, one advantage of laser over optical rangefinders is that they can be used with one hand, as Bill Buckley demonstrates.

In the pictures above and below can you tell just how far it is to those elk? A mature 6-point is a large animal, and hunters often underestimate ranges. A good rangefinder can keep you from shooting at too long a distance.

read the range out to 650 yards—the far side of this particular field. If you're going to sit in one place and shoot for an afternoon, this works.

But unless you own a willing teenager (anybody seen one lately?) or can afford a hunting butler, a four-foot rangefinder is tough to haul around while deer hunting. Hunting models are much smaller; the most popular for rifle shooters is the foot-long Ranging 400. The maker claims that this model measures distances out to four hundred yards. I owned one years ago and wasn't too impressed, but for the purposes of this book I got hold of a brand new model and tried it out one spring day.

I wandered around the countryside, trying the Ranging 400 on various animate and inanimate objects. Out to 100 yards it was accurate to within about five yards, certainly enough for handgun or muzzleloader hunting. From 100 to maybe 225 yards, it frequently showed errors of 10–15 percent. That's still not too bad. For varmint shooting with smaller rounds like the .22 Hornet, and for hunting with most modern "hand rifles" like the Thompson/Center Contender chambered for a rifle round, it would certainly work.

Between 250 and 400 yards I got readings of anything from 250 to 400 yards—but the reading rarely matched the range. Sometimes the rangefinder read 250 yards when the object was 400 yards away, and vice versa. If the target didn't have vertical lines to help adjust the dial precisely, accuracy suffered even more. Ranging does make an 800-yard model, but it's no longer than the 400, which makes me doubt that it works much better.

An alert reader might ask how the heck I knew the Ranging 400 was so inaccurate. Did I survey the country? Did I pace off the distances? Nope. I used a Swarovski laser rangefinder.

Laser rangefinders send a laser beam out to a target, which bounces it back. The tiny fractions of a millisecond it takes the beam to travel back and forth are measured by a computer inside the rangefinder, which translates it into distance. Hand-held hunting lasers are normally accurate within a yard (they're actually more accurate, but that's as close as they're calibrated) out to . . . where? That's the big question.

Laser rangefinders function most reliably when the target is flat, hard, and light-colored. This is called a cooperative target, and most game animals are distinctly uncooperative. Aside from their normal skittishness, they're usually round, fuzzy, and often dark. Laser rangefinders also work best in dim light because there's less outside interference with the laser beam. When a company says, therefore, this magical instrument works out to, say, 750 yards, what does that mean?

In some cases, the rating means the rangefinder is good out to that distance under most hunting conditions. That's the case with the Swarovski. It is supposedly good out to 1,000 yards, but in reality it's calibrated to 999. Anything past that distance still reads 999 in the LED inside the viewfinder. It will read those distances about 80 percent of the time, unless the target is distinctly uncooperative and standing around in the bright light of noon. I have gotten readings, however, off trees (about as uncooperative a target as you'll find) out past 700 yards in bright sunlight, and that's a very long way for any hunter to be shooting at anything.

The design of the Swarovski is similar to most of the hand-held rangefinders on the market. It's about as big as a full-size Porro-prism binocular, and features a 6X monocular for aiming. To operate it, you press a button and an LED reticle appears in the view of the monocular. You place this reticle on whatever you want to, hold the rangefinder steady, and keep pressing the button. Most of the time the range appears on the screen.

The other hand-held laser rangefinder units available as this is written follow the same basic layout. The rated range varies somewhat, as does the magnification in the monocular, but all are about the same size and operate pretty similarly. Sometimes there are other features. The Bushnell, for instance, can eliminate readings at short distances, so nearby brush doesn't confuse the reading on a deer 150 yards away. It has another setting for use in rain or snow, which can also confuse the poor little laser beam. Mostly they all feel, look, and work about the same.

The real differences are in how close they come to their rated yardage. None works quite so reliably under bright sunlight or on noncooperative targets as the Swarovski, so the minimum distance where you'll always get a good reading is maybe one-half to two-thirds the

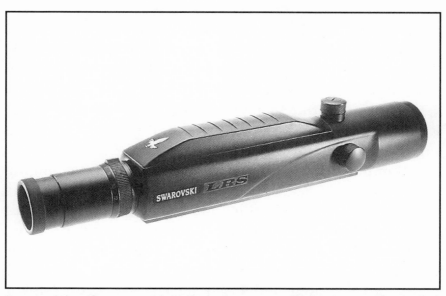

Swarovski's riflescope with built-in laser rangefinder is very heavy and expensive. Most hunters are opting for hand-held rangefinders that can be used with all their rifles.

These West Virginia groundhog shooters are using an old Barr & Stroud military rangefinder. This is practical when you're sitting all afternoon above a hayfield, but not so hot when hiking the hills for big game.

rated range. The Bushnell Yardage Pro 800, for instance, is consistently good only to about five hundred yards. But so what? Even five hundred yards is plenty for any big-game hunting. Since the Yardage Pro's discounted retail price is about $400 versus $3,000 for the Swarovski RF-1 I used in my tests, the Bushnell seems to be leading the market right now.

I emphasize right now because things are changing rapidly in the laser business. Bushnell was first on the market with an "affordable" rangefinder, but for around $250 to $375 you can also buy laser units from Brunton, Simmons, and Tasco. The Brunton is a small design for bow, handgun, and muzzleloading use, rated out to 250 yards, but Simmons and Tasco market 800-yard units for somewhat less money than Bushnell's.

High-Tech Rangefinders

Bushnell is still leading the pack, with a 600-yard unit that will fit in a large hunting coat pocket, and this is the way laser rangefinders will head in the future, despite some other options. I have it on good faith from at least one other major optics firm that a laser rangefinder not much bigger than a pack of cigarettes, able to read yardage consistently out to 600 or more yards and selling for closer to $500 than $1,000, will be on the market within a couple of years, and perhaps by the time you read this.

The options mentioned above include laser rangefinders built into other optics such as Swarovski's 3–12X50 LRS riflescope and Leica's Geovid 7X42 BDA binocular. Both are great instruments with fine optics, and able to consistently read ranges out to 800 or 1,000 yards. But aside from the cost (around $4,500 for the scope and $3,000 for the binocular), there are real disadvantages to each.

The first two are size and weight. Swarovski's riflescope is very bulky and weighs over 40 ounces. That's $2\frac{1}{2}$ pounds, more than three times what the lightest scopes in the 3–10X range weigh. Add one to a 7-pound .30-06 (about the weight of an unscoped Remington 700, Ruger 77, or Winchester Model 70) along with a sling and a magazine full of cartridges, and you'll be packing more than 10 pounds around the hills. I have also heard through the hunting network that they don't hold up too well under the kick of a .300 magnum. Of course, Swarovski will replace the thing if it goes bad, but if you're in the middle of a hunting trip, that's not real possible.

Leica's Geovid is a much more practical tool. A truly fine 7X42 binocular works for about any hunting in the world, and this 7X42 may be the world's finest. Certainly it is second to none, but it weighs just about as much as Swarovski's scope, which is too much to carry around your neck all day.

Of course, as technology lopes along and hand-held rangefinders grow smaller, so will the laser units inside scopes and binoculars. They will have to get a lot smaller before we arrive at a really practical riflescope, and even then, unless you own only one hunting rifle, you must buy another laser scope for each of your rifles. Even if the price winds up below $500 (and it will, since at least one or two Pacific Rim companies will have introduced laser-rangefinder scopes by the time you read this), who wants to go to the expense of scoping three or six or twelve rifles with lasers when one hand-held unit will work with all those guns?

Again, laser-rangefinder binoculars are much more practical. Someday soon we'll probably see really good binoculars, complete with laser, costing under $1,000 and light enough to wear around your neck all day. When that happens, I'll own one. Until then I'll stick with a hand-held unit.

HOLOGRAMS, NIGHT VISION, AND OTHERS

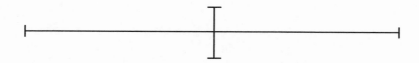

Aside from laser rangefinders, there are other electronic optical devices that can help the hunter—some more than others. Perhaps the most common is the type of sight generically known as red dot. First popularized by Aimpoint and now made by several companies, this type of sight doesn't magnify; instead, it superimposes a glowing red dot on the target.

Most often used in certain target games, red-dot sights do have advantages in some kinds of close-range hunting, particularly anywhere a shot must be taken quickly at a moving target. They're mounted just like scopes, but since eye relief isn't critical, they can be mounted well forward. These days most are built on very short 30mm tubes but normally come with mounts, including an extension to cope with the short tube. Since the typical red-dot sight weighs only a few ounces, even with mounts they rarely add more than half a pound to a gun.

In hunting, perhaps the best use for red-dots sights is on a shotgun—and not necessarily a slug gun. Slug guns

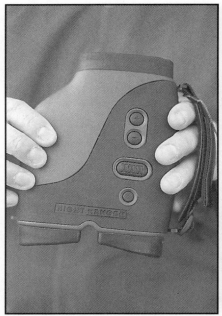

The author is puzzled about exactly how night-vision scopes can be used in hunting. About their only real use is for making your way to a stand in the dark, without alarming game by using a flashlight.

are normally used for deer and black bear, and hence can definitely benefit from the extra brightness a standard rifle scope provides. Red dots, on the other hand, are best mounted on scatterguns for wingshooting.

It may seem very odd to add optical sights to a bird gun, but legendary gunwriter Jack O'Connor more than once described Bill Weaver's use of a 1X (no magnification) scope for wingshooting, saying Weaver was "undoubtedly the best quail shot I have ever hunted with."

The first red-dot sight I ever saw in action was mounted on an Ithaca 10-gauge semiautomatic shotgun owned by my late friend and hunting partner, the outdoor writer Norm Strung. Among other things, Norm was a waterfowl addict, and when the Aimpoint people first showed him one of their units, his eyes lit up. About that time Ithaca brought out its semiauto 10-gauge. Norm was an old 10-gauge user, so he bought an Ithaca, mounted an Aimpoint, and went forth to slay Canada geese.

This was back before nontoxic shot regulations, and over the years Norm had perfected large-shot, 10-gauge handloads. Norm noted how large the red dot appeared next to a goose at various ranges, and used it as a rangefinder. By the end of that season he was crumpling Canadas at ranges unheard of since the days of Idaho gunwriter Elmer Keith.

Strung's and Keith's ideas about the amount of lead a Canada goose needs at ranges out to seventy-five yards matched almost exactly, and I saw Norm consistently—not just occasionally and luckily—drop big honkers at that range. (When I hear of somebody putting down Elmer Keith's tales of long-range waterfowling, I just smile.) The mandating of steel shot reduced those ranges, of course, but with the perfection of bismuth and the recent introduction of tungsten shot, big geese can again be cleanly killed at long range.

In 1996, Bushnell introduced another non-magnifying aiming device called the Holosight. Unlike the red-dot sight, which uses a lighted reticle combined with a prism system, the Holosight's reticle is a split-laser hologram.

Unlike laser rangefinders (and the laser sights commonly used on defensive handguns), this laser does not send a beam out to the target. Instead, it builds a hologram in the Holosight's screen. Holograms are technological illusions. The shooter sees the apparently three-dimensional image of a reticle way out there next to the target, as far away as he can see the target.

Unlike scopes and, to a lesser extent, red-dot sights, the field of view and eye relief of the Holosight are almost unlimited. Your eye does not have to be lined up exactly behind the Holosight to see the reticle. I suspect that with practice a left-eyed, right-handed shooter could confidently shoot a Holosighted shotgun from his right shoulder, and parallax is eliminated at any angle where the reticle can be seen.

One of the two biggest problems for any shotgunner is keeping the cheek on the stock each and every time. (The other is slowing or stopping the swing. Unfortunately, the Holosight can't help that.) When skilled gunners miss, it's often because they didn't "keep their head down." With a Holosight, you can crane your head around like a giraffe: If the sight is on the target, so is the shotgun.

I used a Holosight on a scattergun—my old Remington 870—for the first time during an early spring shooting session with a portable trap. The reticle was a small dot surrounded

Bushnell's Holosight is a marvelous shotgun sight, especially for long-range shooting.

by a circle that subtends sixty inches at one hundred yards. After sighting-in on a snowbank (the Holosight adjusts like a scope, with dials for elevation and windage), I tried a few straightaways, placing the dot on the target and pulling the trigger. All the clays broke, including birds that dropped steeply when a side wind gusted. Many of us lift our heads to get a better look at falling birds and consequently shoot high. With the Holosight, I held the top edge of the reticle's circle on the clay and broke every one.

On crossing shots, the edge of the circle worked out to a perfect lead. I swung the dot through the bird, until the trailing edge of the circle touched the clay target, and pulled the trigger. Despite 20-mph gusts, I broke the last dozen in a row.

I primarily shoot real birds, and normally miss more than one or two clays out of, say, twenty-five. (As Elmer Keith pointed out, clays slow down and start dropping after taking off, the opposite of most gamebirds.) Consequently, my sporting clays shooting, while something I will perform in public, is full of misses on down-angling clays. With the Holosight, which allowed me to see exactly where the reticle was when the gun went *bang*, I began to understand how I missed those shots.

For a beginning shotgunner, the Holosight helps even more. My friend Bill McRae, the noted big-game writer and photographer, claimed he'd never been able to "hit a bull in the butt" with his own 870. Bill is by no means a shotgunner. Once, we were hiking along a small creek looking for a good spot to take some posed hunting photos when a pair of mallards took off. Bill watched them fly and said, "Now, how can you shoot those beautiful birds?"

I said, "You've got to lead them."

So Bill is not a shotgunner. But he helped me test the Holosight that first day, and broke more than half the clays he shot at.

Soon afterward I carted my Holosighted 870 to another informal clay-bird session. At the shoot were three beginning shooters who, despite a couple of lessons, could not hit much of anything with double-barreled shotguns that supposedly fit them very well. They were discouraged, which was not good either for them or the future of shooting.

So I handed them the 870, gave a little instruction on where to hold the reticle, and let them *whang* away. Within three or four shots each shooter was hitting clays regularly—and at that point every one of the three started to giggle. They were having real fun with a shotgun for the first time. By the end of the shoot, they had a good feel for the swing and timing of the shot, and were able to make the transition to their more traditional shotguns.

Even some experts could find use for the Holosight. I can't imagine a better pass-shooting waterfowl gun than a 12-or 10-gauge semiauto mounted with a

The various red dot sights work very well for short-range rifle, handgun, and shotgun shooting, but in much hunting the extra brightness of even a low-power scope works better. Plus, most scopes don't need batteries.

Holosight. At sixty yards you know exactly where that pattern will land.

The Holosight doesn't provide the brightness of a good scope, but it also works fine for quick, short-range handgun and rifle shooting. One afternoon I had the opportunity to shoot one of Freedom Arms's superb .22 magnum revolvers at ground squirrels on a Montana ranch. Because of the revolver's fine accuracy, sighting-in was easy (I hesitate to report the groups I shot at fifty yards, because I normally can't shoot a rifle much better). The rig worked very well on the "gophers" out to about seventy-five yards. I think the revolver was up to longer ranges, but I simply couldn't see most of the squirrels any farther away. A gray-brown Columbian ground squirrel in gray spring sagebrush doesn't show up too well if he isn't moving.

One model of the latest Holosight features 2X magnification, which helps a little bit, but the screen actually dims the world slightly. The best way to use one, as with a red-dot sight, is with both eyes open; consequently, the non-magnifying model seems more practical.

I haven't been nearly as impressed with that other recent high-tech hunting aid, night vision. When night-vision scopes (which are not sighting devices like riflescopes but rather seeing devices like spotting scopes) first appeared on the market, there was a great hue and cry about poaching and other illegal uses. I really can't see how they could materially help a jacklighter, mostly because the view is so grainy.

The first scope I tried was the Bushnell model. It is an amusing toy. You can walk around your house and yard at night with all the lights off and see. The view is not exactly Technicolor, since everything comes out green, black, and white, but you can indeed walk around in the dark without stumbling over sleeping dogs, barbecues, and the other objects that litter the night.

You'll also see some wonderful special effects. Night scopes work by enhancing any particle of available light, and from my upstairs window I could see lights occasionally sweeping across the hills beyond my lower pasture. These hills are more than half a mile from the house, and it took a few minutes to realize that the lights were the headlights of cars coming over another hill two miles away.

The scope failed miserably, however, in revealing any detail beyond a few yards. From the same window I can see about 120 yards down to my benchrest, back in the corner of the same pasture against a line of willows and alders. This benchrest is about the size of a deer, and even though I knew it was there, I couldn't see it. I could see the brush, but that was it.

To me night scopes are interesting playthings but of limited use for hunting, or even poaching. You certainly couldn't locate deer much past fifty yards with one. One friend suggested that a poacher could find deer in the night scope, and then switch on a regular spotlight for the shot, switching the spotlight off as soon as the deer dropped. This would allow less time for a game warden to see the telltale beam of the spotlight. Maybe. I doubt it.

One night-scope promoter showed just how ignorant he was by saying he'd used his to guide his horse to camp after dark. Gimme a break. A horse can see better in the dark than any human with a night scope, especially when the hunter has seen the countryside only in daylight, and knows the way back to camp already. Believe me, even your yard looks very different when seen in grainy green and white.

Maybe you can negotiate a mountain trail using a night scope, but the best use I see for one is boating. I sure could have used a night scope on a canoe trip in West Virginia. We got caught by darkness a mile short of the bridge where we were supposed to be. That last mile was navigated at first by looking for the faint gray of whitewater, but after the first twenty minutes we avoided rocks only by trying to heed the sound of the river washing over them. A night scope would have been handy there, or maybe in a duck boat. I suspect a big flashlight would work as well or better.

As for as locating game in the dark, big binoculars or a really big spotting scope do the job much better than any night scope. Notice I said locate, not shoot. I do a lot of my scouting with optics, and once in a while it's a great help to find game just before first light, so you can start the stalk in the dark. This doesn't apply only to deer, elk, or other timber game. A couple of years ago, I found a buck antelope in my Pentax binocular long before shooting light. He was walking along a stand of cottonwoods on the edge of a stock dam, and I followed him in the 10X42s until he stopped to graze on a flat beyond the trees more than half a mile away. Could I have seen him better through a night scope? In a word, no. I couldn't have seen him at all. Until somebody builds the definition of binoculars into night scopes, they will always be toys in the woods.

FUTURE AND PAST

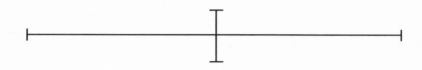

Where will hunting optics go in the future? Things will change with improved technology. We'll see more stabilized binoculars, smaller and more accurate laser rangefinders. Scopes and binoculars will become even brighter and sharper—and probably cheaper. Already optical engineers are making glass that differs in density throughout the lens. Instead of the traditional doublet—two lenses of different densities held together by clear glue—one lens will do the same job. So there will be two fewer glass surfaces to diffract light, and more light will make it to our eye. We'll also probably see some combination of quality binocular and night-vision device.

What do all these technological advances mean for the hunter? Hunting is at its heart a rather atavistic undertaking. Though still perfectly valid as a way of gathering food, hunting is for most of us much more than a search for food. We hunt to reconnect with the wild in a time when other technologies—computers, airports, cellular phones—constantly conspire to lock us firmly into a world that is increasingly man-made.

So as hunting optics inevitably "improve," will the elemental act of hunting be affected? In this last decade of the twentieth century, hunters have spent more time debating hunting ethics than in all of the rest of the century. There is a very good reason for this—machines, and the machine mentality, have invaded hunting.

Of course, this started long before we even evolved into Homo sapiens. The process of humanity's hunting has been the story of technology, from the instant we decided to try a more diverse diet than fruit and grubs and picked up a rock to brain an antelope. From there we started chipping at rocks, and it wasn't long before we attached a chipped rock to a branch to make an ax or spear.

From there hunting technology sailed along, through the atlatl, bow and arrow, crossbow, and hunting gun, which itself has seen thousands of technological improvements over the centuries. Humans can't even leave the old technologies well enough alone—as witness the strange things that have happened to the bow in the last thirty-odd years.

And those are only the essential hunting tools that we use to bridge the gap from a human's hand to a deer's heart. Today's hunters also have Gore-Tex, polypropylene underwear, all-terrain vehicles, propane camp stoves, two-way radios, and even electric eyes that tell us when and how often deer pass in the night.

Today we have rifles accurate enough to place all their bullets into a deer's heart at 600 yards, with 20X scopes that can be adjusted for range. I used a .243 with just that kind of scope to shoot prairie dogs off a rancher friend's cattle pasture last summer. Toward noon the rancher drove by and watched for a half-hour, during a period when I just happened to make a string of shots out to five hundred yards. Not just one or two lucky hits but several fully intentional shots.

"Man," he said, shaking his head. "You sure won't have any trouble killing a deer at six hundred yards this fall!" I looked at him for a few seconds, pleased at the compliment to my shooting, but then said I wouldn't shoot at a deer that far away. He looked puzzled and asked me why not.

My answer involved judging wind and the fact that a prairie dog hit with a .243 would instantly die, no matter where the bullet landed. Either they were hit and killed, or they were missed entirely. If I misjudged the effects of range and wind on a six-hundred-yard deer, however, the deer might suffer a nonfatal wound, and that just wasn't right. But the reason went deeper than that. It went back to the essence of hunting.

Is it hunting when we ride the hills in an ATV and shoot game startled by the sound of an internal combustion engine? Is it hunting when we see a distant antelope, measure the range with a laser, dial in 547 yards on our 15X scope, and try a shot? Is it hunting when technology takes the place of physical effort and knowledge of game?

Many people believe that hunters crossed a line somewhere back there in the inexorable march of technology. Since hunting technology includes items like Inuit mukluks, the poisoned arrows of !Kung Bushmen, reproduction flintlock rifles, compound bows, computer-designed binoculars, and Nosler Partition bullets, the exact location of that line is highly debatable.

At the heart of all real hunting lies something already alluded to, and that is knowledge of the game. When our technology negates almost any need to learn about the wild animals we hunt, then we're no longer hunting. Just what we're doing I don't know, but hunting it is not.

Many of today's hunters embrace every technological advance they can buy, which is why many "primitive weapon" seasons have become races to the next muzzleloading or

Are huge variable scopes and ultra-velocity magnums necessary for hunting? Its gotten to the point where many hunters think a lever-action with a 4X scope is a "primitive" weapon. If you hunt with your binoculars and feet, the author's .250 Savage works fine even in the wide-open badlands of eastern Montana. His handload, a 115-grain Nosler Partition at 2,700 fps, did the job admirably on this mulie doe at 150 yards.

bowhunting gadget. That race is the reason some states are beginning to ask whether an in-line muzzleloader—equipped with a modern scope, firing saboted handgun or even rifle bullets, with fake blackpowder pellets at velocities impossible for any flintlock—is really primitive.

A very few states and agencies saw all this coming early on. Pennsylvania makes sure everybody really uses a primitive weapon during their muzzleloading seasons by outlawing all muzzleloaders except flintlocks and any sights except iron. A buddy of mine who works for the Lolo National Forest here in Montana said they outlawed all-terrain vehicles on everything except public roads a decade ago. They could see the future, in which every mountain would become a highway and any attempt to cut back on the traffic would result in howls from the citizens who'd just spent several thousand dollars on ATVs. In some places, ATVs have replaced legs (and knowledge of the game) to such an extent that I have seen more than one "bowhunter" blow an elk bugle while sitting on an idling ATV.

It is quite literally human nature to invent and try new technologies. That's how the Inuit and !Kung survived in the extremes of their harsh environments: They invented tools to cope with ice and desert. Far from being antitechnological, both societies are perfect examples of the human mind and hand constructing easier ways to live.

So what's this all have to do with hunting optics? Unlike the low-tech tools of Inuit and !Kung, much modern technology removes the human mind from the hunting equation. Yes, humans invented all the marvelous tools we use, such as binoculars and laser rangefinders, but it wasn't the average hunter who did so, and abusing such tools doesn't improve either the art of hunting or the public's view of the hunter.

So where do we draw the line? Many hunters are going back to real muzzleloaders like sidehammer flintlocks, or cartridge guns with iron sights. Others not quite so dedicated, or perhaps not blessed with youthful eyesight, have turned to older or simpler optics.

As should be obvious by now, I believe in optics for hunting. I hunt more than occasionally with iron sights (especially good peep sights) but believe that within the correct context, scope sights are highly ethical. They allow us to place our shots more precisely, which results in cleaner kills. They allow us to really see our game, even in the often dim light of forests and deep canyons, and not shoot mistakenly at an illegal deer, somebody's dog or horse, or another human being.

Sure, scopes are abused by some shooters, who "try" shots at distances far beyond their skills. They're abused even by fine shots who evidently believe that spending time and money on an expensive hunting trip grants them permission to shoot at uncertain distances and any angle. These are the same people who believe that the guide they hired will help track down the wounded animal they have paid so much to claim. Sure, scopes are abused by some, but scopes also make the shot of a hunter who has stalked within one hundred or two hundred yards much more certain.

I have also thought long and hard about laser rangefinders. These are more likely to be abused than scopes, but used properly I believe they are also fine hunting tools. Instead of making longer shots possible, however, they should eliminate the common mistake of shooting too far. Bill McRae carried a Bushnell laser rangefinder while hunting grizzlies in Alaska a couple of years ago. He and his guide saw a big grizzly across a valley and stalked within a few hundred yards. The guide urged him to shoot, but Bill was convinced the range was much farther than his self-imposed limit of two hundred yards for grizzly shooting, so he used the rangefinder to measure the range—which turned out to be much closer to three hundred yards than two hundred. They stalked closer, and Bill killed the grizzly cleanly with one shot from his .375 H&H at just under two hundred yards.

I normally don't carry a laser rangefinder, instead using my scope's reticle to measure distance to familiar game. Unlike deer, pronghorns, and elk, however, bears come in all sizes, and that's where the use of a laser rangefinder is most appropriate. On the other hand, it is neither appropriate nor ethical to use a laser rangefinder as an aid in shooting antelope at eight hundred yards, as a man I once guided was fully prepared to do. He had a brand-new .300 Winchester Magnum, and when we first saw the herd, he sat down and ran a round into the chamber. Very quickly I suggested stalking closer. He said he'd bought the magnum so he didn't have to do all that damn walking! (No, he did not shoot at those distant pronghorns. I threatened to spook them if he tried. We stalked to within 250 yards, whereupon he missed.)

I don't know how you feel about all this, but most of the hunters in my circle hunt with plain old fixed-power scopes of no more than 6X, and often only 2½X or 4X. Why? Because then they feel they're hunting, not sniping.

In fact, there's a growing segment of the hunting world that is beginning to regress a little—not all the way back to longbows and flintlocks but to cartridges like the 7x57 Mauser, wooden stocks, and 4X scopes. These really aren't handicaps as big as most gun and hunting magazines would like you to believe.

Because of my profession, I have hunted with the finest optics in the world. One of the perks of the job is getting invited on expense-paid hunting trips all over the country, and even to exotic locales around the world in Canada, South America, and Africa. Because my hosts often want me to "field test" new equipment, I've hunted with lots of high-tech optics, from super-variable, range-adjustable scopes to laser rangefinders.

For my personal hunting in Montana and other nearby states, simpler appeals more to my senses of ethics and esthetics. I don't really have much use for variable scopes on my general hunting rifles. The only big-game rifles in my rack that wear variables are chambered for calibers that may also be used on very small targets (either edible small game or agricultural pests such as prairie dogs and coyotes) or big rifles that may be used on dangerous game. These have low-power variables in the 1–4X

Some hunters who prefer the advantages of scopes but object to the long-range obsession of much modern hunting are starting to use old scopes and rifles. From top: a Model 20 .250 Savage with a 2.5X Noske scope in an Echo side mount; a Model 99 .250 Savage with a 2.5X Lyman Alaskan in a Stith mount; a Remington Model 30 in .30-06 with a 2X Weaver 330 in old "straddle"-style Weaver mounts. All will do the job quite neatly out to 250 yards, which is about all that's needed if the hunter knows how to use binoculars.

to 1.5–6X range, or removable 4X scopes and easily available iron sights.

My rifles in calibers like .270, 7x57, and .30-06 all have fixed-power scopes. I haven't felt any particular handicap when hunting with them, perhaps because I almost never take a shot over three hundred yards. If you can't kill a deer cleanly at three hundred yards with one of today's 6X scopes on a .270 (or even a 4X scope on a 7x57), then you need more practice, not more scope or rifle.

A growing segment of my gun rack is filled with even more "primitive" tools, such as a lever-action .250 Savage with a 2X Lyman Alaskan, and a 7x57 Ruger #1 single-shot with a 3X Weaver. I have killed game as large as elk with bows and muzzleloaders, but in middle age I more clearly appreciate the certain killing power of smokeless cartridges. Combine these with traditional rifles and small scopes, and I can use the skills I developed with truly primitive weapons and still kill game as cleanly with modern bullets.

For some hunters an eating-size mule deer stalked across four hundred yards of sagebrush, then killed at seventy-five yards with an old lever gun, provides far more satisfaction than a much bigger buck sniped at five-hundred yards with a .300 magnum and a 4–12X scope. For some hunters the essence of *trophy* changes as we grow older. I have some big heads on the wall, but as the decades roll by I have found they kindle memories of the hunt rather than provide any ego satisfaction. So now I hunt more for memories than heads, and simpler rifles refine the memories of stalks through sagebrush and ponderosa.

For similar reasons, more and more hunters are beginning to collect old binoculars and scopes. Over the years I've noticed that the less time hunters can spend in the field, the more time some like to spend gathering and fooling with their hunting tools. Some carve duck decoys or gunstocks, while others collect fine old shotguns—or even optics. Buying used optics is a whole world in itself, and because the dealer vultures haven't taken over the market as they have with pre-'64 Model 70 Winchesters and double rifles, prices can be quite reasonable.

If you know how to shop, there are some fine bargains in used hunting optics. There are still few hunting binoculars better than the 1950s-era Bausch & Lomb Zephyrs, one of the first lightweight Porro-prism models with multi-coated lenses. Though they are somewhat dimmer than modern scopes, there are few better hunting scopes than the old Lyman Alaskans, Noskes, and the best of the steel-tube Weavers. These are the prizes of hunters yearning for simpler times. In the past decade, I've watched the price of Alaskans and old Weavers rise from maybe $35 to $100 or more.

Even modern scopes and binoculars can often be purchased very cheaply on the used market. Optics do not hold their value like firearms do. A new rifle may cost $500 and, if still in good condition, sell for $400 a year or two later. Most optics drop 30 percent to 50 percent in price once you leave the store, and sometimes much more.

There really isn't much to buying used optics. You might peruse old *Gun Digests* or other catalogs to see which brand sold for the most in 1956. Back then the European and American economies were more similar, and price was a better indication of sheer quality than it is today. Then check out the optics section of the *Gun List* to see what's desirable today.

I have picked up a lot of my old optics in pawn shops and at gun shows and yard sales. After taking a look through the lenses, I shake 'em. A good shake reveals any loose lenses, adjustments, eyepieces, etc. If the seller doesn't want you to shake 'em, that says something important. Place that old scope gently on the table and walk away. If I hear no rattles or musical glass, I look carefully around the edges of the lenses. This is where many old scopes and binoculars take a beating, and they sometimes stay together even with a severely edge-chipped lens. Old steel-tube Weavers seem particularly vulnerable in the objective area; I've seen several that looked perfect in every other way but on close examination showed cracks or even loose lenses.

Leupolds hold their value more than any other used scope, except maybe some of the European brands (which, if you haven't figured it out by now, I consider somewhat overpriced), and some discontinued Leupolds can be had at very decent prices. I particularly like the older 4X scopes. These are just as rugged and light as Leupold's new 4X, which is a fine scope but not long enough to be mounted for correct eye relief on many lever or single-shot rifles. The company's old 6X compact was also a hell of a scope, as bright as anybody really needs, but very light and just the right size for mountain rifles. If you run across a Bausch & Lomb Balfor compact 4X, you've found one of the very brightest, toughest 4X scopes ever made.

If you really get into old scopes, you should also carefully consider tube diameters and mounts. One friend traded for a very fine old 4X Kollmorgen (the forerunner of Redfield), only to find it had a 26mm tube. The only source I know for 26mm mounts since Redfield went out of business is Conetrol. Weaver makes rings for 7/8-inch scopes, and Conetrol makes shims that allow you to mount 7/8-inch scopes in 1-inch rings. In your search for vintage optics, you'll need to remember that the diameters of some old scopes are very weird, and mounts simply may not be available. You might be able to find a gunsmith who can ream out 1-inch rings or make shims for 30mm rings, but it might be more trouble than it's worth.

Used spotting scopes can also be great bargains, though many of the older models are much heavier than the newer stuff and rarely come with adjustable eyepieces. More likely you'll find a scope with a 20X or 25X eyepieces or maybe two eyepieces, one of 20X and other 30X or so.

You may also need to have old optics repaired. A number of folks specialize in this service, though they seem to be mostly older men. Sometimes correspondence and repair can be slow, and one who did work for me is now in that big optics-repair shop in the sky. I'd look in the advertisements of gun magazines, then ask pointed questions. Many repair specialists can perform or sub-contract even such technically demanding jobs as recoating lenses, but given the prices and time involved, sometimes it's easier just to locate another old scope or binocular and buy that.

If you're also into old guns, another item beginning to get hot on the used market is scope mounts, especially the old Stith mount that was designed to fit already existing holes and slots. These were usually for $7/8$-inch, straight-objective scopes like the Lyman Alaskan. With an old Alaskan and a Stith mount you can often scope that undrilled pre-'64 Model 70 or Savage 99 without destroying the collector's value. The S&K and B-Square companies also make mounts that fit without drilling or tapping, especially for military rifles.

You might also end up collecting old books about sporting arms. With the help of my several old books, I've been able to figure out exactly when a certain Noske scope was made, and that the Weaver 330 on my 1930s-vintage Remington .30-06 probably was installed at the factory. (Yes, rifle/scope combos were sold even back then.) Plus, the books themselves often increase in value over time. All of these endeavors—collecting, reading, hunting—give us some appreciation of our own hunting history, something that is always valuable, on several levels.

At its most basic, it just may prevent you from adopting the modern perspective of an Alaskan guide I hunted with a couple of years ago. Early one morning we'd taken a jet boat up a shallow river, then climbed a hill and glassed for giant moose. We saw several, two miles away across a muskeg flat at the base of a long mountain. We hadn't been finding any in more accessible (or perhaps I should say "sane") places since the season had opened three days before, so we packed up our spotting scopes and ran down the hill to the jet boat, zipped across the river, and started through the bankside alders. We'd taken about ten steps when the guide turned and whispered, "If we jump a bear and he charges, don't shoot until I do!"

This was probably a sensible legal idea, the guiding laws being what they are in Alaska (and many other places, for that matter), but perhaps not truly practical, for my guide was carrying his custom .30-378. This in itself is not too bad a brown-bear cartridge. But the rifle had a 26-inch barrel topped with a big muzzle brake, a thumbhole stock with a big hooked pistol grip, and a 6.5–20X Leupold scope.

Now, the guide may have been able to get that thing trained on a charging brown bear in those alders, but I doubt it. The longest distance we could see until we broke out onto the muskeg was about fifty feet, and most of the time we couldn't see half that. Much of the time we couldn't have swung any sort of long gun. I nodded, but if a bear hassle arose, I was betting on my battered old .338 Mauser with its 22-inch barrel and plain old 4X scope.

We did not run into a bear, which was just fine with me, and I didn't get a moose, either. Mostly we got some awkward aerobic exercise in the muskeg, and a few mosquito bites. That evening we did find a bull caribou on another hill. We stalked within three hundred yards, whereupon I said I could kill the bull. The guide wanted to get closer because of my puny scope, but there wasn't much cover left, so I lay down, rested my rifle on my day-pack, and put one 210-grain Nosler through the caribou's heart. A little historical perspective would have greatly eased my guide's mind in both cases.

Here's to seeing clearly, both historically and optically. Good hunting!